The Voice...

Hearing the Almighty

The Voice...

Hearing the Almighty

Batya Ruth Wootten

The Voice... Hearing The Almighty

by Batya Ruth Wootten

© 2009, Batya Ruth Wootten, Saint Cloud, FL.

Cover by John Diffenderfer, Artistream, Lebanon, TN, 615.547.1555. www.artistream.info

All rights reserved under International and Pan-American Copyright Conventions. To use or reproduce any part of this book, electronically or otherwise, written permission must first be secured from the publisher. Brief quotations with credits may be used in critical reviews or articles.

Published by: Key of David Publishing, PO Box 700217, Saint Cloud, FL 34770 407.344.7700.
www.keyofdavidpublishing.com

Distributed by: Messianic Israel, PO Box 3263, Lebanon TN 37088 800.829.8777
www.messianicisrael.com

Printed in the United States of America.
All quotations used by permission.

Unless otherwise noted, Scripture quotations are from the *New American Standard Bible* (NASB), © 1995, The Lockman Foundation, published by Holman Bible Publishers, Nashville; and the *New New American Standard Bible*, Quick Verse for Windows, © 1992-1999, Craig Rairdon and Parsons Technology; © 1998 by Electronic Edition STEP Files, Parsons Technology, Inc. Cedar Rapids, Iowa.

Verses marked KJV are from the *King James Version* Bible.

Verses marked NRSV are from *The New Revised Standard Version With Apocrypha*, © 1998 by Electronic Edition STEP Files, Parsons Technology, Inc. Cedar Rapids, Iowa.

Verses marked NIV are from the *New International Version*, © 1995 by The International Bible Society, published by Zondervan Publishing House, Grand Rapids.

Note: To emphasize some Scriptures, italics or an alternate word choice has been used, especially for the names of the Father and Son. Also, brackets [] indicate text added by the author.

ISBN 1-886987-27-0

Dedication

To all who long to hear the voice of the Almighty and be obedient to His voice. May we be given ears to hear and a heart that longs to obey only Him.
Shema Yisrael...

In Appreciation...

Special thanks to Hale Harris, General Secretary of the Messianic Israel Alliance, who graciously allowed us to reproduce his telling article,
"The Idolatry of the Intellect."
Thanks also to retired school teacher, and friend, Merle Rawlings, who allowed us to reproduce his encouraging message,
"The Best Is Yet to Come!"
We also offer our deepest thanks to all who helped with this work...

"...In the latter days you will return to the Lord your God and listen to His voice" (Deuteronomy 4:30).

YHVH – יהוה

We use these four letters to indicate the Name of the One True God, which is often mistranslated as "the LORD." Jewish tradition has avoided its use. The Creator's Name is actually comprised of four Hebrew letters, יהוה, yod, hey, vav, hey, and is variously translated: Yahweh, Yahveh, Yahvah, Yehovah, or Jehovah, etc. We will use the four English letters that best duplicate the sound of these Hebrew letters (as pronounced in modern Hebrew), YHVH. In this way, the reader can determine if and how it is to be pronounced. YHVH was sometimes called by the diminutive "Yah" (יה) which we will also use (Psalm 68:4). Also, one of His titles, "God" (*Elohim* in Hebrew), will sometimes be used.

Yeshua – ישוע

Yeshua is the Messiah's given Hebrew/Aramaic name. It means "Salvation" (Mat 1:21). Jesus is derived from a Greek rendering of Yeshua: Iesous. They changed His name because their language did not have a "sh" sound, and because they added an "s" to the end of male names. This Greek transliteration was converted into English, at a time when the English letter "J" had a sound like that of today's "Y." The name was thus pronounced "Yesus," much like the Greek name. However, with the hardening of the sound of the English "J," it began to be pronounced as "Jesus." We therefore choose to transliterate the Messiah's name from Hebrew into English, as "Yeshua."

Ephraim – אפרים

Ephraim is the name of Joseph's second son and means "doubly fruitful." This name was used by the Ten Tribes of the Northern Kingdom, also known as the Kingdom of Israel. The term "Ephraimite" was sometimes used to describe those of this Northern Kingdom of Israel (as opposed to the Southern Kingdom of Judah). The Ephraimites lost their identity when they were exiled by the Assyrians (around 722 B.C.). We will use this name to describe those known as the "Ten Lost Tribes" and to broadly speak of non-Jewish Believers in the Messiah of Israel (Gen 41:52; 48:19; 2 Ki 17:34; 1 Ki 12:21; Isa 8:14; Eze 37:15-28).

TORAH— תורה

Torah means teaching, instruction, direction, but is often translated as the "Law." YHVH says He loved Abraham because he kept His Laws (Gen 26:5). Abraham kept the spirit of the Torah before the letter of it was given to Moses. Everyone who wants to be a success should likewise look to our Father's precepts for guidance. Moses said of them, "Keep and do them, for that is your wisdom and your understanding in the sight of the peoples who will hear all these statutes and say, 'Surely this great nation is a wise and understanding people'" (Deu 4:5-6). King David said, "How blessed are those whose way is blameless, who walk in the Law of YHVH. How blessed are those who observe His testimonies, who seek Him with all their heart. They also do no unrighteousness; they walk in His ways.... Oh that my ways may be established to keep Thy statutes! Then I shall not be ashamed" (Psa 119:1-6).

As New Covenant Believers, we are saved by grace through faith, not by works, but by the shed blood of our Messiah, and by the word of our testimony. It is with this understanding of all that our Messiah has done for us, and of the wise and simple faith of our forefather Abraham, that we speak of honoring the wisdom of Torah.

Contents

- Foreword xv
- Preface xix

Chapters

1. *Shema....* 1
2. The Voice Within 7
3. Our Patriarchs Heard.. 15
4. The Great Voice 21
5. Forever Chosen to Choose 27
6. A Recap: Who Should Hear? 33
7. The Essence of the New Covenant 37
8. The Sheen and the Spirit 39
9. Last Days Dangers 47
10. The Idolatry of Intellect 49
11. Lawlessness and a Renewed Commandment . 55
12. Making A Commitment 61
13. The Best Is Yet to Come! 69
14. Voices in Scripture 77
15. *Kol ba'Midbar* 85
16. Whispers and Shouts 97
17. The Road to Zion... 105
18. *Ha Kol Shel Abba* 111

- Study Helps 113
- Bibliography 125
- Biography 129
- Key of David Publications 131

FOREWORD

The Creator of the Universe is speaking to us. As a people called to be a *mamlechet kohanim v'goy kadosh*, a "kingdom of priests and a holy nation," we must hear the God of Israel. He wants to lead us and guide us. He wants us to fulfill our potential as "sons of the Living God" (Hos 1:10; Rom 9:26). We hear His voice ever more clearly as we align ourselves with His Kingdom and His ways. Batya Wootten understands this, and as one of the founders of the Messianic movement, she has a prophetic calling to bring the Body of Messiah back to a sure foundation. One of these foundations is the essentiality of hearing and obeying the voice of God.

In the pages of scripture, we read that God speaks to individuals about specific things they are called to do. Think about this for a moment: where would we be today if Abraham had not responded to God's call to leave Ur of the Chaldeans? What if Moses, Joseph, Gideon, David, or a host of others, had not heeded the voice speaking to them?

The Voice... Hearing the Almighty

The heroes of faith were people just like you and me. They chose to listen and obey, and as a result, they did extraordinary things. YHVH has a job for you to do as well. We're part of the same story of redemption and restoration, and we continue what they established.

Communication is the essential quality of any healthy relationship. Do we really think it was God's plan for us to relate to Him exclusively through an earthly priest or pastor, religious rules and regulations, or a book? Even the ultimate, Spirit-inspired book, the Bible, has a goal in mind: God wants us to learn how to relate to Him as a person, the eternal Being who is our loving Father. But various religious systems, and the mindsets underlying them, have confused the issue of how we relate to God. Oftentimes, these systems serve as substitutes for the glorious and intimate relationship we were always intended to enjoy. They inoculate us from catching the real thing— which is a walk of power and intimacy, and worship in spirit and truth. The real thing transforms us and the world around us. The call of every generation, and especially the final generation, is to bring us back to the true gospel.

All around us, we see the fruit of moral relativity and humanistic thinking. We expect it from secular society, but it has permeated the Body of Messiah as well. Are we truly qualified to serve as our own gods? Do we recognize the full implications of that ancient lie: "Ye shall not surely die: For God doth know that in the day ye eat thereof, then your eyes shall be opened, and ye shall be as gods, knowing good and evil" (Gen 3:4-5).

Are we truly submitted to the voice of the one true God? The most basic definition of sin, according to Isaiah 53, is turning to your own way. "All of us like sheep have gone astray, each of us has turned to his own way; but the LORD has caused the iniquity of us all to fall on Him" (vs. 6). Sadly, even many believers go their own way, or the way

FOREWORD

of other religious people. Matthew 7:21-23 reveals the tragic consequences of this deception. In the end, there will be many who did things in God's name; yet, God did not "know" them. We must both hear and obey. *Shema Yisrael!*

The wilderness was a difficult place for Israel, and the wilderness of life is no less difficult for us. It destroys some and purifies others. Wouldn't it be great to have a personal guide and mentor who would strengthen and instruct us along the way, a person who will teach us, encourage us, and make us better people? That is precisely what we do have, if we will just believe it.

Is there anything more awesome than hearing the voice of God? Recognizing and submitting to the voice of our personal guide, the Holy Spirit, is what separates the overcomer from those who fail. We must enter into this greater dimension of intimacy and obedience. It is a great blessing to do so.

The prophet Ezekiel saw a valley full of dry bones which represented the whole house of Israel (Ezek 37). Ezekiel was told to prophesy to these bones, and as he did so, God's Spirit came forth to resurrect this ancient nation. They rose to their feet and became an "exceedingly great army." An amazing vision, but we must ask the question, has this great event come to pass? Or does Israel still defile themselves with their idols, detestable things, and transgressions?

My dear friend, Batya Wootten, has always had a burden for both houses of Israel. I believe she is among those who are being raised up to intercede in the same way Ezekiel did. It is her desire that Israel would repent and return to their God, and in doing so, recognize one another. This burden was placed in her by the Spirit of God, and her specific calling and life's work is to write and speak prophetic words.

The Voice... Hearing the Almighty

The people of Israel will rise to their feet in the end of days. They will be an army of people doing the right thing; an army of people exercising their specific gifts and callings in grateful response to the grace of God; an army of people serving and loving each other. They will hear the Voice and respond.

If you want to be part of that army, reading this book will help you in your quest.

Hale Harris
General Secretary
Messianic Israel Alliance
President
B'nai Ephraim International
Fishing Guide, Co-Owner
Bighorn Trout Shop
www.bighorntroutshop.com

PREFACE

Scripture speaks of a "period of restoration of *all things* about which God spoke by the mouth of His holy prophets" (Acts 3:20-21).

"All things" would include our ability to hear the voice of our Creator— as did Adam when in the Garden.

YHVH said, *in the last days*, the children of Israel will return to Him and listen to His voice (Deu 4:30).

We surely live in the last days, which means it is now time for Israel to learn to listen to, and obey, His voice. But, if the prophecy is about the children of "Israel," what does it have to do Messiah's non-Jewish followers?

The answer is, "Everything." This verse is especially important to them.

For decades now, my husband, Angus, and I have sought to help Believers to see "both the houses of Israel," as defined in Scripture (Isa 8:14). We write with an understanding about *all* Israel— Ephraim and Judah.

We have long taught about the *melo hagoyim*, "the fullness of Gentiles" Jacob prophesied would come from

Joseph's son, Ephraim (Gen 48:19; Rom 11:25). We have taught in detail about Israel's Northern and Southern Kingdoms and about how the Father is now making their two houses, and their companions, "one stick in His hand" (Eze 37:15-28).

At this time, Believers from around the world are returning to their Hebraic roots. In the process, many are seeing the truth about *all Israel*. They are seeing that Jesus, or *Yeshua* (His given Name in Hebrew), is the Messiah of all Twelve Tribes of Israel. [a]

So, what does our understanding about Ephraim and Judah have to do with hearing the voice of the Almighty?

Much in every respect.

Almost everyone agrees that in the last days, the focus of the God of Israel is on the restoration of the house of Israel. In this hour, we need to see that He is reuniting the "two sticks," as prophesied in Ezekiel. YHVH is making regathered Israel "one stick" in His mighty hand. Thus, if we do not have a fundamental understanding that Israel was long ago divided into two houses, we will be hindered in realizing her restoration process. We will not see the Father's present goal. We will not understand how He wants to use both houses in this day and hour.

As for using us, in order for each of us to truly know what He wants *us* to do, *as individuals*, we must learn to hear His voice for ourselves.

As for hearing Him, His word for us at this time is, "Not by might nor by power, but by My Spirit" (Zec 4:6).

---

[a] We use *Believer* to describe those who follow Messiah Yeshua rather than *Christian*, because the latter is often misused (Mat 7:23; 1 Cor 6:20; 1 Pet 1:17-19). We use *Yeshua* (ישוע), because it is the Messiah's given Hebrew name. It means "Salvation" (Mat 1:21). When transliterated into Greek, due to linguistic differences, *Yeshua* became *Iesous* (Ιησους). In Old English, "Iesous" was then rendered "Iesus" (pronounced *Yesus*), and was spelled with a beginning letter "J," which at the time had a "Y" sound. Later the "J" came to have a harder sound, and it came to be pronounced as "Jesus." Since this name is the result of linguistic differences, we prefer to use His given Hebrew/Aramaic Name, Yeshua.

PREFACE

Man, in all his might, simply will not be able to get us where we need to go. "For not by might shall a man prevail" (1 Sam 2:9).

We cannot do what needs to be done in this hour apart from the Father's Holy Spirit. We also will not understand what the Father wants to accomplish if we do not understand His plan for the restoration of the whole house of Israel. To be kept safe in this hour, we truly need to learn to hear His saving voice for ourselves.

This book is therefore a heart-felt prayer, a plea, a cry for Messianics especially to realize the imperative truth that we will not see Israel's restoration apart from or without the Ruach haKodesh. ᵇ It is written especially to those of the Messianic faith, to those who desire to return in power to their Israelite roots. It issues a clarion call for Believers everywhere to arise, to realize our need to hear our Father's voice, according to the truth of the Scriptures—from Genesis to Revelation.

Batya Wootten
Saint Cloud, FL

---

b For more information about the Holy Spirit and how He works in the Body of Messiah, please see the book, *Israel– Empowered by the Spirit*, by Wallace E. Smith and Batya Ruth Wootten, 2009, Key of David Publishing, Saint Cloud, FL.

The Voice... Hearing the Almighty

SHEMA...

SHEMA...

One word from the Almighty can change things in the twinkling of an eye. It can make things different in an instant. Moreover, hearing from Him is vital to our faith, even crucial to our well-being.

Our challenge is to learn to hear a *sure* word from Him. Our difficulty is in knowing for certain that we are actually listening to *His* voice, and not to that of another...

For various reasons, man tends to fear hearing the voice of the LORD. Yet, many promises in Scripture speak of the Father's people ultimately learning to hear His voice and thus to walk in His blessings. Scripture tells of a time when Israel is empowered to both hear and obey His voice. Through Moses He says to us, *"In the latter days you will return to YHVH your God and listen to His voice"* (Deu 4:30).

This promise has to do with the "latter days," so it probably applies to the time in which we now live. At the very least, the time for its fulfillment must be getting close. It also speaks of people who are *returning* to the God of Israel. So who are these returning ones?

The Voice... Hearing the Almighty

Return is here translated from the Hebrew root word, *shuwv*. Isaiah similarly uses this word, saying, "The redeemed of the LORD [YHVH] shall *return*, and come with singing unto Zion; and everlasting joy shall be upon their head: they shall obtain gladness and joy; and sorrow and mourning shall flee away" (Isa 51:11). [1]

This promise gives rise to several questions: To whom is it given? How should it affect their walk? And, what does it mean to listen to the voice of YHVH our God?

To fully appreciate the meaning behind this promise, we need answers to these inquiries. We begin with the last question first: What does it mean to *listen* to His voice?

Sadly, most of us feel like we have "heard" the voice of our God at some point in our lives, only to later discover that we were led astray by our own carnal thoughts. Most of us also have, on occasion, been misled by the compelling voice of a man or even been deceived by the voice of the evil one.

In this world many voices clamor for our attention. Yet the one voice we all need to hear is that of the Almighty. Again, we are commanded to "listen to His voice," and we are warned that we will perish if we do not listen to Him (Deu 4:30; 8:20).

Listen is here translated from the Hebrew word, *shema*—it being the first word in the ancient declaration of faith of the Jewish people:

> *Sh'ma Yisrael Adonai Elohaynu Adonai Echad.*
> Hear, Israel, the Lord is our GOD, the Lord is One. (Deu 6:4). [2]

---

[1] *Strong's Hebrew and Greek Dictionaries*, and *Brown-Driver-Briggs Hebrew Lexicon* (Electronic Edition, STEP Files © 1998, Parsons Technology, Inc., Cedar Rapids), word # H7725: shuwb or showv). (Hereafter, *Strong's*; when referenced together, *S&BDB*.)

[2] Judaism uses the title *"Adonai"* or "Lord" in this prayer in deference to the proper Name of the Holy One, which they do not use, lest they take it in vain. A more accurate reading of the text might be, "Hear, Israel, YHVH our *Elohim* is One YHVH." *Elohim*, or *Lord*, is a title that is often translated "God." The actual *name* of our God is יהוה, or YHVH. *YHVH Elohim* is often translated as "LORD God."

SHEMA...

HEAR AND OBEY

The first thing we must realize about the command to *listen* to Yah's voice is that *shema* is a verb— an *action* word. It means to hear intelligently, to listen with attention and interest, then to obey. [3]

Thus, to truly hear a command of the Almighty means we will in turn respond to and obey His command. When we hear His voice we are obligated to respond with respect to what we hear. We cannot separate the idea of action from the Hebrew *shema*. Furthermore, doing nothing is a decision. Inaction is a form of action— and lack of action results in negative consequences (Rev 3:15-16).

We are to yield to the voice of the Almighty, then act according to His instructions. If we refuse to obey His voice when we hear it, we risk being like those whom He called "stiff-necked and rebellious" (Neh 9:17).

It is not just ancient Israel that had this problem. In the New Covenant we read, "Therefore, just as the Holy Spirit says, 'Today if you hear His voice, do not harden your hearts as when they provoked me, as in the day of trial in the wilderness'" (Heb 3:7-8).

Today, in the moment when we hear the voice of the Spirit, it is important that we quickly respond, lest we too, be called "stiff-necked."

When we do listen to YHVH's voice, we invariably find that what we heard was actually for our own good.

I DID, OR DIDN'T, LISTEN TO THE VOICE

Surely there are as many testimonies as there are people who have felt they heard a voice within themselves telling them to do something, yet they did not give it proper regard and thus missed an opportunity:

---

[3] *S&BDB* word # H 8085.

The Voice... Hearing the Almighty

"I wish I had listened" the story usually goes. "Things would have been so different..."

"If only I had not taken the car when my father told me that the roads would probably be icy."

"I wish I had listened to my mother's advice, but no, I felt I knew so much more than she did. Now I'm in a real mess."

"I thought I was supposed to go to that school, but I let my friend talk me out of it. Attending it would have been much better for my career."

We also hear of, know of, or even are, one of those who heard a voice within and thankfully, we did listen:

"I am so glad that I responded to the sense of reservation that I felt," the story goes. "If I had bought the tickets, I would have been in that plane crash."

"I am so glad that we went to look at those houses, even though at first they seemed to be so far away. Now we live here and love the neighborhood."

"I am so glad that I went to the meeting because I met my husband there," or, "...I met my wife there."

The lists go on forever. Each of us has surely had this type of experience many times in our lives. Without exception, when we do hear the voice of the Holy One speaking within us, we are better off if we listen to Him.

We must realize that the Almighty says of each one of us, "'I know the plans that I have for you,' declares the Lord, 'plans for welfare and not for calamity to give you a future and a hope'" (Jer 29:11).

The King James renders this verse, "I know the thoughts that I think toward you, saith the Lord, thoughts of peace, and not of evil, to give you an expected [or, *hopeful*] end."

The New International Version reads, "'I know the plans I have for you,' declares the Lord, 'plans to prosper you and not to harm you, plans to give you hope and a future.'"

The Tanakh translates the text as, "I am mindful of the plans I made concerning you— declares the LORD— plans for your welfare [shalom], not for disaster, to give you a hopeful future."

As we seek to learn about the voice of our God, we can trust in and listen to Him, because He only wants to build us up and not tear us down (Pro 3:5). He wants us to live in perfect peace, in absolute *shalom*— which word means, to live safe, well, happy, and in peace. [4] This is true, even if we are in the midst of dire circumstances.

Our Father in Heaven wants us to prosper, to have a sense of well being, to have hearts that are filled with hope. No human eye has seen, no ear has heard, no mind has even conceived of the wonderful things He has in store for those who love Him (1 Cor 2:9).

When our loving Father speaks to us, when He seeks to woo us to Himself, we hear words that help establish our well being. Thus we would do well to always listen to Him. We would do well to stop doing all the talking and learn to quietly listen. He is always saying, "Be still and know that I Am God" (Psa 46:10, KJV). "Cease striving," He says.

Listen.
Be still.
Let Him speak.

---

[4] *S&BDB # H7965.*

The Voice... Hearing the Almighty

THE VOICE WITHIN

Two

THE VOICE WITHIN

The Hebrew word for voice in Scripture is *kol*. [5] The word is first used in Genesis 3:8. There we read that Adam and Eve "heard the *voice/kol* of the LORD God walking in the garden in the cool of the day: And Adam and his wife hid themselves from the presence of LORD God amongst the trees of the garden" (KJV).

As we know, Eve listened to the voice of the serpent, ate of the forbidden fruit, then offered a bite to Adam. In turn, Adam, who had earlier been told not to eat of the tree, by "The Voice," by the Almighty Himself, chose instead to listen to the voice of his wife.

Adam acquiesced, ate, and then, realizing that he and his wife were naked and being in fear of their Creator, they hid from Him. Thus, the Father said to Adam,

> "Because you have listened to the voice of your wife, and have eaten from the tree about which I commanded you, saying, 'You shall not eat from it'; cursed is the

---

[5] *S&BDB* word # H 6963.

ground because of you; in toil you will eat of it all the days of your life" (Gen 3:17).

Adam's problems started when he revered the voice of a mortal above that of his Creator. This was Adam's first sin— and it is the root of our problems too. Adam was thus led astray, and we all tend to follow in his foolish footsteps. We listen to the voices of men and are often led astray from our ordained path. More importantly, we tend to fear hearing the voice of the Almighty. But why so?

Fearing the Voice of the Almighty
Preferring the Voice of Man

The thunder and lightning that accompanied the voice of the Holy One as it was heard from Mount Sinai was so awesome that the terrified children of Israel said to Moses, "Speak to us yourself and we will listen; but let not God speak to us, or we will die." [6]

Although the Holy One wanted to speak to them from Heaven itself, they preferred to have His life-giving words delivered to them by a mortal man (Exo 20:18-22).

We see this same tendency when Israel cried out for a king. They were being governed by the God-ordained prophetic voice of Samuel, but when it became apparent that his sons were not following his ways, instead of demanding righteousness from them, the people cried out, "Give us a king, so we can be like the other nations."

In response to their request, YHVH said to Samuel, "Listen to the voice of the people in regard to all that they say to you, for they have not rejected you, but they have rejected Me from being king over them" (1 Sam 8:7).

---

6 The Torah was given through "disposition of angels" (Deu33:2; Acts 7:53; Gal.3:19; Heb.2:2). The words *thunderings* and *lightning* (*kole* and *lappeed*) can also mean *voices* and *torch/fire* respectively. Scott Skaggs, Messianic Israel Talk 07/05/08.

The Voice Within

When YHVH spoke to the sons of Israel, they saw no form. They preferred a visible mortal with a human voice over the awesome voice of their unseen God (Deu 4:12).

YHVH warned Israel of what would happen to them if they listened to the voice of a mortal king. He warned that men would use them and their goods for their own gain. But the people refused to listen to His word through Samuel. They said, "There shall be a king over us, that we also may be like all the nations, that our king may judge us and go out before us and fight our battles" (1 Sam 8:4-20).

Such has been our sin from the time we left the Garden. We have feared hearing the voice of our invisible Creator and have preferred the voices of visible mortals. And we do it because we want to be like the other nations...

Testing the Heart

Listening to the voice of a Spirit God surely requires certain disciplines from us. In order to be able to listen to Him we must:

- Learn to differentiate between His voice and that of our own
- Realize that our human hearts have the capacity to be very deceitful, even to ourselves (Gen 8:21)
- Know that only the Holy One truly knows the heart. He says, "I search the heart, I test the mind, even to give to each man according to his ways, according to the results of his deeds" (Jer 17:9-10)

Learning to embrace Yah's testings tests our mettle.

We know that He is all-knowing, and He tests us, not to learn what we think, but so we can see for ourselves the wickedness that lies in the recess of our own hearts. In His mercy, He shows us these things that we might have opportunity to repent during our sojourn here on earth.

The Voice... Hearing the Almighty

He does this because we can repent in this life, but can only give an account of our lives in the next life. So, we want to know the truth about ourselves now— while we can still do something about our mistakes.

As for truth, we do not want to think we know the truth, yet be deceived, but instead want to truly hear the truth, and we want to hear it from the voice of our Father.

Hearing His voice can frighten and test us because hearing Him in turn begs the question, *Will we obey His unseen voice— especially if the request seems out of the ordinary?*

YHVH tested Abraham when He spoke to him about offering his only son Isaac on an altar. And, because Abraham obeyed the voice that he heard, YHVH said, "In your seed all the nations of the earth shall be blessed, because you have obeyed My voice" (Gen 22:1-18).

When ancient Israel was crying out for water in the wilderness, the Father tested them saying, "If you will give earnest heed to the voice of YHVH your God, and do what is right in His sight, and give ear to His commandments, and keep all His statutes, I will put none of the diseases on you which I have put on the Egyptians; for I, YHVH, am your healer" (Exo 15:23-26). [7]

For the sake of our own well-being we need to learn to hear and obey the voice of the Holy One.

So why is that so hard for us to do?

The Spirit Voice Within

In his book, *Astrology, Psychology, & Religion: Revisited*, Dr. Atlas Laster makes a suggestion that, if correct, could alter understandings of our call here on Earth. It could help us better understand the purpose of our life in this world. He suggests that after Adam sinned, for the first time, he heard the voice of the Holy One *outside* of himself.

---

[7] See also Exo 16:4; Deu 8:16; Jer 20:12.

THE VOICE WITHIN

Laster writes:

> "Shortly after the original sin, Adam and Eve began to understand what it meant to be disconnected from Yahweh. Originally, man heard from and communicated with the Creator directly and immediately within self through the union of spirit-to-Spirit. After sin, there was a different relationship between man's spirit and Yahweh's Spirit. For the first time, as shown in Genesis 3:8, Adam and Eve heard Yahweh's Spirit as something distinctly outside themselves, something they had not heard previously: 'And they heard the voice of the LORD God walking in the garden in the cool of the day....' The newness of what they heard engendered a strange earthly, fleshly, reaction. They became afraid, aware of their nakedness, and hid....."

Laster offers several rabbinic quotes with similar interpretations of Genesis 3:8 that essentially agree the sound was "unlike any sound they had ever heard before." [8]

Getting the Voice Back Inside...

The primary point of the Garden of Eden escapade is that Adam knew he was *naked* (Gen 3). [9] However, this additional, incredible insight suggests that YHVH's voice was initially heard *within* Adam's being. Adam became separated from the voice of the Holy One after his disobedience and fall; then YHVH's voice was heard outside man. Adam hid from the voice of the Holy One, and man has been having problems with properly hearing the Almighty ever since that time. We need to truly hear, and not gloss over this profound truth.

---

[8] *Astrology, Psychology, & Religion: Revisited*, Atlas Laster, Ph. D., page 34, B'Sod Yesharim Foundation, 2002, St. Louis.
[9] Note: *Naked* is rooted in the Hebrew word for *cunning*. Adam became like the cunning one who deceived him. See *S&BDB* word #'s H 5903; 6191; Gen 3:1.

We were surely created to be spirit-dominated beings, led by the voice of our Creator, which voice was meant to be heard *within* ourselves. We were initially designed to communicate with Him, *spirit-to-Spirit*. But, Adam became *naked*. This word is rooted in the Hebrew word for *cunning*, which is used to describe the Serpent (Gen 3:1; footnote 9). Adam began to be like the one who deceived him, and thereafter, man's soul was dominant. Man became sense-oriented: our physical senses, our soulish-selfish desires became the preeminent factors in our lives.

As Believers in Messiah who have been born anew of the Holy Spirit, we do not want to put an inordinate focus on body and soul but, instead, want the dominating force in our lives to be that of the Holy Spirit. However, this often leads to difficult, hard-fought spiritual battles. It is as Yeshua told His disciples, "Keep watching and praying that you might not enter into temptation, because the spirit is willing, but the flesh is weak" (Mat 26:41; Mark 14:38).

The flesh is weak in regard to honoring the things of our God, yet it is often strong as it pulls us in the wrong direction: "The flesh sets its desire against the Spirit, and the Spirit against the flesh; for these are in opposition to one another, so that you may not do the things that you please." Thus, we are told to, "Walk by the Spirit, and you will not carry out the desire of the flesh" (Gal 5:16-17).

We learn to walk by the Spirit through *training*. "Solid food is for the mature, who because of practice have their senses *trained* to discern good and evil." *Trained* has to do with *naked practice*. And, we are *"laid bare* to the eyes of Him with whom we have to do" (*Strong's* G1128; Heb 4:13; 5:14). In other words, the truth of our inner man is exposed, and through practice, our senses learn to recognize Abba's voice as opposed to our own carnal voice.

YHVH communicates with us, Spirit to spirit— not so much in words, but in thoughts and impressions. Our goal is to demolish arguments and pretension that arise against the knowledge of God. Our objective is to take captive our every thought and make it obedient to Messiah. Thus, our flesh must die on a daily basis: "If you are living according to the flesh, you must die; but if by the Spirit you are putting to death the deeds of the body, you will live. For all who are being led by the Spirit of God, these are sons of God" (2 Cor 10:5; 1 Cor 15:31; Rom 8:13-14).

To understand YHVH's Spirit, we note that Isaiah speaks of "The Spirit of wisdom and of understanding, the Spirit of counsel and of power, the Spirit of knowledge and of the fear of YHVH" (Isa 11:2, NIV). These facets of God can be seen in the following diagram. In it, we see a man with a candlestick, or *menorah* in the center of his being, and a menorah-like pattern above it, with the facets of the Spirit as listed by Isaiah. If we read the matching branches in Hebraic form, which is from right to left, we find that:

- When we fear/revere YHVH, we gain understanding
- When we have knowledge of the Word (Yeshua), we gain wisdom
- When we receive the counsel of the Ruach, we gain strength

In this way we also see Father, Son, and Holy Spirit.

In summary, after the fall, it appears that the voice of our God was outside man rather than within him. And, the further away we get from having His voice within us, the more lost we become. The further away we get from hearing His voice, which is like the sound of many waters, like the comfort of cleansing rain, the more we flounder in the tumultuous seas of life.

Life on earth is about getting the voice of our Beloved back within us. It is about us learning to once again communicate with Him. It is about our being led by His *Ruach haKodesh*.

The Voice... Hearing the Almighty

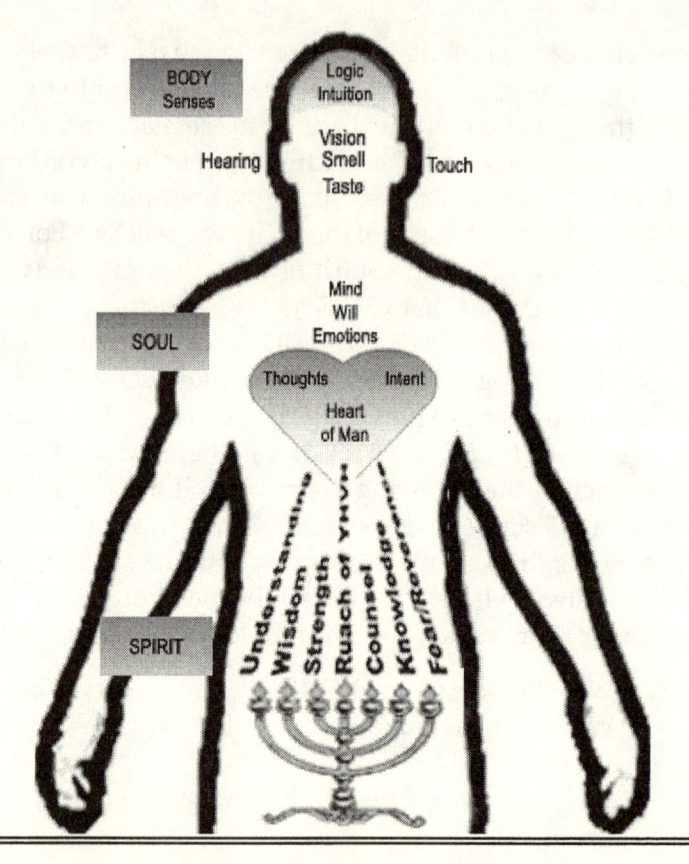

BODY Senses: Logic, Intuition, Vision, Smell, Taste, Hearing, Touch

SOUL: Mind, Will, Emotions, Thoughts, Intent, Heart of Man

SPIRIT: Understanding, Wisdom, Strength, Ruach of YHVH, Counsel, Knowledge, Fear/Reverence

Knowing God

We do not want to focus on the things of the world but on the things of the Spirit. We want to put away the cares of this world and have our hearts filled with the purposes of the Holy One of Israel. We want to be led by His sevenfold Spirit (as outlined in Isa 11:2).

When we follow that menorah-like pattern and read the matching branches first right, then left, then right again, and left..., we find:

When we fear/revere YHVH, we gain understanding.
When we have knowledge of the Word (Yeshua), we gain wisdom.
When we receive the counsel of the Ruach, we gain strength.
Thus we see Father, Son, and Holy Spirit in Isaiah 11:2.

Chart by Batya Ruth Wootten. Graphic and idea from the book, *"Sons to Glory"* by Paul Jablonowski: www.sonstoglory.com. Used with Permission.

Three

Our Patriarchs Heard...

The human voice is an amazing thing. According to science, no two of the billions of human voices found in the earth are exactly alike. Like fingerprints, each human voice has a distinct pattern. Yet, beyond basic categories (like high, medium, low), the many differences found in our unique voices is difficult to define or describe.

Our forefather Isaac tried to distinguish between human voices when his wife Rebecca and their son Jacob planned to deceive him. The story reveals that Isaac was going to give the firstborn blessing to the wrong son, and Rebecca knew it. Isaac did not listen to the voice of his wife, who had warned him that he was going to give the blessing to the wrong child. As a dutiful helpmeet, which might be likened to a "Divine Radar System" that ever warns of danger, Rebecca respectfully voiced her objections to her husband. And if she was like most wives, she probably voiced them on more than one occasion...

Sarah had to do the same thing with Abraham. He was going to give his firstborn blessing to Ishmael rather than

The Voice... Hearing the Almighty

to their son, Isaac. So she similarly warned her husband of the reservation she felt in her spirit. [10]

It appears that these women were trying to hear and obey the voice of the Holy One. As for Rebecca, whatever the reason for her objections, we see that she devised a plan. She instructed Jacob to take some stew to his father and to pretend to be his brother Esau. Then, when Jacob came close to Isaac his father, Isaac felt him and said, "The voice is the voice of Jacob, but the hands are the hands of Esau" (Gen 27:22).

Isaac discerned the voice and thought it was not what it claimed to be. But rather than go with what he discerned, he trusted in the arm of the flesh and decided instead to follow his feelings. Perhaps Yah (YHVH) allowed Isaac to be deceived in this case because he would otherwise have made a serious mistake by not choosing the son whom Yah had chosen. So He allowed intervention in the matter.

Trusting in the arm of flesh leads to trouble. Going with what feels right, following human feelings, can lead to deception. Like Elijah, we must listen to the gentle, still, small voice (1 Ki 19:11-13). We begin by listening to our conscience, which is divinely equipped with an innate sense of right and wrong, and is always either accusing or defending us in our actions (Rom 2:15).

Again, our goal is to learn to hear the voice of the Almighty for ourselves. YHVH blessed Abraham because he obeyed His voice. Abraham is even called the father of all who believe— because he listened to, and obeyed, the voice of the Almighty (Gen 22:18).

Abraham Believed the Voice

"Abram." The voice that called out the name of our forefather had a sound like that of many waters.

---

[10] See *Mama's Torah: The Role of Women* by Batya Ruth Wootten, 2004 (Expanded Edition: 2009): Key of David Publishing. Saint Cloud, FL.

"I am going to bless you," the majestic voice continued.

"Lord," Abram inquired, "How can I receive Your blessing if I do not have a child that comes from my own loins? You have given me no offspring; my only heir is a Gentile named Eliazar— a steward born in my house."

"Your servant," said the Lord, "Shall not be your heir. Only one that shall come from your inward parts— only an heir from your own body shall inherit your blessing."

"Come out here, Abram," the Lord invited. "Look up at the stars and count them if you can. If you can count them, you will know the number of descendants that will come from your loins in fulfillment of My promise to you."

Abram stepped out of His tent and looked up at the clear night sky. He could see no end to the stars. Nor was there an end to the comfort he found in the voice of the Lord. Abraham smiled, and his body, though soon to be a century-old, straightened as he looked to the sky. "There are myriads of stars," he thought. "Myriads," he said as he turned around and around, looking up. "Myriads..." (see Gen 15:1-6).

Abram's name was later changed to Abraham to reflect the fact that he would one day be "the father of many nations." Abraham believed God would do what He said He would do and give him numerous physical descendants. And, the Almighty credited that faith to Abraham as "righteousness" (Gen 17:5; Rom 4:3).

Isaac Was Directed By The Voice

Isaac was walking a dusty road that would lead him to Gerar and King Abimelech. Even as his father had gone to Egypt during the previous famine, so now he followed in the footsteps of his father. Then he heard it...

"Do not go down to Egypt," the voice called out to Isaac.

Isaac knew it was the God of his father, so Isaac listened

as the voice continued, "Though the land is suffering famine, I will be with you and your offspring and I will establish with you the oath I gave to your father, Abraham. And, I will increase your offspring like the stars of the heavens."

Isaac trusted that the One whose voice he heard would both protect him and greatly multiply his descendants, so Isaac settled in Gerar (see Gen 26:1-6).

JACOB TRUSTED THE VOICE

An awesome voice called out to Jacob, "Arise, go to Bethel, and live there; and make an altar there to God."

Then God appeared to Jacob again when he came from Paddan-aram, and said to him, "I am God Almighty; be fruitful and multiply; a nation and a company of nations shall come from you, and kings shall come forth from you. And the land which I gave to Abraham and Isaac, I will give it to your descendants after you." Then God went up from the place where He had spoken with him.

After hearing the plan for the multiplication of his seed (it being the blessing given to his fathers), Jacob believed the LORD, and named the place where God had spoken with him, *Bethel*, meaning, *House of El* (see Gen 35:1-13).

THEY ALL HEARD THE VOICE...

Abraham, Isaac, and Jacob, all heard a voice that sounds differently from all others. They heard the voice of our God speak great and mighty words of blessing over them. They heard mysterious words of almost unfathomable promise, and each of them believed and acted upon those words.

Like our forefathers, we too need to hear and obey the voice of our God. We also must believe His promises. We must believe Him when He says, "Call to Me and I will answer you, and I will tell you great and mighty things, which you do not know" (Jer 33:3).

Our Patriarchs Heard...

The Voice of Messiah Yeshua

Adam heard the voice of the Almighty and regularly communicated with Him in the Garden. Moreover, we are told that Messiah Yeshua came to restore that which was lost. What was lost is that, in the cool of the evening, our God walked and talked with Adam (Gen 3:8-9).

Messiah came to restore mankind's lost ability to have personal communication with the Almighty. That is why Yeshua said His sheep "hear His voice" and follow Him. Messiah said He calls each of His sheep by name, they respond to His voice alone, and will not obey the voice of a stranger. He also said that those who are "of the truth" hear His voice (John 10:3-5,16,27; 18:37).

Yeshua did not say His followers *might* or *could* hear His voice, but that they *do* hear His voice. Therefore, if we are not hearing His voice, it is *not* because He does not want to communicate with us. Perhaps we do not hear because we are not truly listening. Possibly we are too busy, and He does not speak in busy-ness, but in quietness. Elijah found that in turbulent times, YHVH was not found in a strong wind, an earthquake, nor in fire, but in "a still small voice" (1 Ki 19:13-12; Psa 46:10; Isa 30:15).

We must learn to be like a radio receiver and trust that our God is ever transmitting encouraging words of comfort that will lead and guide us. Moreover, hearing and obeying His voice serves as proof of our restoration. Hearing Him gives testimony to the fact that we are found members of Messiah Yeshua's formerly lost sheep (Ezek 34:11). Hearing His voice is vital to our restoration. It shows that He has found us and that we have found what was once lost. We simply cannot overstate the importance of hearing, and obeying, the voice of our God— especially in this hour.

Again we note that Adam and Eve "heard the sound of YHVH Elohim walking in the garden in the cool of the day" (Gen 3:8). The Hebrew word translated "cool" is rooted in the word for *Ruach*, as in *Ruach haKodesh, the Holy Spirit*. [11] Adam and Eve walked in the Garden, *in the Ruach*, with YHVH Elohim. We need to do likewise.

To Live in the Land of Milk and Honey We Must Listen to YHVH's Voice

There is great reward in hearing and obeying the voice of the Almighty. And, serious consequences come with not listening. The sons of Israel walked forty years in the wilderness until all the men over age twenty perished. That happened "because they did not listen to the voice of YHVH" (Josh 5:6). So it is that not listening to the voice of the Father will keep us out of the Promised Land:

> "This is what I commanded [your forefathers]... 'Obey My voice, and I will be your God, and you will be My people; and you will walk in all the way which I command you, that it may be well with you.' Yet they did not obey or incline their ear, but walked in their own counsels and in the stubbornness of their evil heart, and went backward and not forward. Since the day that your fathers came out of the land of Egypt until this day, I have sent you all My servants the prophets....Yet they did not listen to Me or incline their ear, but stiffened their neck; they did evil more than their fathers" (Jer 7:22-26).

When we do not immediately respond, listen to and obey (*shema*), the voice of the Almighty, we are walking in the footsteps of the faithless ones of Israel. The warning is, "*Today,*" if you hear his voice, do not harden your heart and provoke Him (Heb 3:7-8). When we believe and quickly respond to His voice, we are following in the righteous path of our faithful patriarchs.

---

11 *S&BDB* # H 7307.

Four

The Great Voice

YHVH spoke burning words to the twelve tribes of Israel at Mount Sinai. Of these words, Moses said:

> "These words YHVH spoke to all your assembly at the mountain from the midst of the fire, of the cloud and of the thick gloom, with a great voice, and He added no more. He wrote them on two tablets of stone and gave them to me.
>
> "And when you heard the voice from the midst of the darkness, while the mountain was burning with fire, you came near to me, all the heads of your tribes and your elders.
>
> "You said, 'Behold, YHVH our God has shown us His glory and His greatness, and we have heard His voice from the midst of the fire; we have seen today that God speaks with man, yet he lives. Now then why should we die? For this great fire will consume us; if we hear the voice of YHVH our God any longer, then we will die. For who is there of all flesh

The Voice... Hearing the Almighty

who has heard the voice of the living God speaking from the midst of the fire, as we have, and lived?"

YHVH said to Moses, "'I have heard the... words of this people which they have spoken to you' ....Oh that they had such a heart in them, that they would fear Me and keep all My commandments always, that it may be well with them and their sons forever!

"...I...speak to you all the commandments and the statutes and the judgments which you shall teach them, that they may observe them in the land which I give them to possess. So you shall observe to do just as YHVH your God has commanded you; you shall not turn aside to the right or to the left. You shall walk in all the way which YHVH...has commanded you, that you may live and that it may be well with you, and that you may prolong your days in the land which you will possess" (Deu 5:22-33).

Hearing the Voice That Burns

Jacob's heirs did not want to be led by the voice of the Holy One but, instead, wanted to be like the other nations; meaning, they wanted to have a visible king who would tell them what to do. So YHVH allowed them to have King Saul— but He first warned them that they would be sorry for choosing the voice of a man over His voice (1 Sam 8).

Abba (Daddy) wants to be able to communicate with us, yet man tends to be more comfortable taking instructions from the voices of fellow mortals. The children of Israel were afraid to hear His voice when He thundered in the Sinai. "Why should we die?" they said to Moses.

"This great fire will consume us; if we hear the voice of YHVH our God any longer, then we will die" (Deu 5:25).

The Israelites said they heard YHVH's voice from the midst of a "fire," or *aysh* (vs 5:24).

THE GREAT VOICE

Yah's voice is sometimes described as burning, fiery, flaming, hot. [12] This is so because the words He speaks have the power to burn away the dross in man.

Moreover, His is a burning voice that, one day, mankind will no longer be allowed to ignore:

> "Behold, the name of YHVH comes from a remote place; burning is His anger and dense is His smoke; His lips are filled with indignation and His tongue is like a consuming fire; His breath is like an overflowing torrent, which reaches to the neck, to shake the nations back and forth in a sieve, and to put in the jaws of the peoples the bridle which leads to ruin... [and He] will cause His voice of authority to be heard" (Isa 30:27-30).

THE REFINER'S FIRE

We are told that YHVH "will sit as a smelter and purifier of silver" (Mal 3:3). We see what this means through a story about a lady who once visited a silversmith and asked if he would please explain to her the process of refining silver.

Watching the man at work, the lady asked why he carefully watched as the silver was being refined, never leaving it. He told her that if the time necessary for refining were exceeded in the slightest degree, the silver would be injured. She then asked how he knew when the process was complete. His reply was, "When I can see my own image in the silver, the refining process is finished."

Similarly, for the sake of our purification, our God sometimes has to put us into a furnace. [13] But, His watchful eye is ever on us during these times. In His wisdom and love, He knows what is best for each of us; and He knows exactly how much heat we can actually bear.

---

12 *S&BDB* word # H 784.
13 He especially purifies Levi's sons, so their offerings will be righteous: Mal 3:3-4.

Our God does not allow random trials. He is always carefully and purposefully burning away *only our dross*.

We must trust that He will not allow us to be tested beyond what we can endure, and that, His end purpose is to have us reflect the image of our Messiah to the world: "For those whom God foreknew, He also predestined to become conformed to the image of His Son, so that He would be the firstborn among many brethren" (Rom 8:29).

The Word reveals that, "the refining pot is for silver and the furnace for gold, but YHVH tests hearts" (Pro 17:3).

YHVH chastens those whom He loves...

Discipline and Sonship

YHVH corrects us because He wants us to be everything He knows that we are capable of being. "I am with you... to save you...[and] will chasten you justly." Even so, we are told: "Blessed is the man whom You chasten, O Lord, and whom You teach out of Your law" (Jer 30:11; Psa 94:12).

Proverbs tells us "a fool rejects his father's discipline, but he who regards reproof is sensible" (Prov 15:5). Thus, it is foolish for us to reject our Father's discipline.

YHVH disciplines His sons— with diligence: "Those whom the Lord *loves* He disciplines. ... He scourges *every* son whom he receives. ... He disciplines us for our *good*, so that we may share His *holiness*." Therefore, we must not think of discipline as rejection, nor think those who do not endure correction are preferred. According to Scripture, "If you are without discipline, of which all have become partakers, then you are illegitimate children and not sons" (Deu 8:5; Pro 13:24; Heb 12:6,8,10).

Discipline is a mark of true sonship. All sons will endure YHVH's rod of correction at different times in life. Lack of discipline indicates a loss of hearing on our part. If we hear Him at all, we will surely hear Him lovingly correcting us.

Perfect Love Casts Out Fear

We should not fear hearing YHVH's voice, because He is *love* and *perfection*. "There is no fear in love...perfect love casts out fear." We fear when we think we are going to be punished: "Fear involves punishment, and the one who fears is not perfected in love" (Col 3:14; 1 John 2:5-6; 4:8-18).

Fear of hearing the Father's voice possibly suggests we previously resisted His voice and spurned His correction. If so, we need to go back to that point of rejection and openly and humbly repent. Fear also can indicate that we do not really know Him. We may know *about* Him and have intellectually accepted His existence, but we have never made Him the LORD of our life. If so, we need to repent of our sins and ask Him to come into our heart and take up residence there (Rev 3:20-22). Fear indicates that we need to be perfected in His love. The presence of fear reveals that we do not know in our heart that eternal punishment no longer awaits us when we die.

One secret to being delivered from fear is found in the verse, "We love, *because He first loved us.*" Hearing of Yah's love for us and learning that Messiah Yeshua paid the required price for our sins by washing them away speak of that unending love. When we know, firsthand, His matchless love for us, we no longer fear Him. If we have fear, we need to return to the basics: "For God so love the world, that He gave His only begotten Son..." (John 3:16).

Walking in YHVH's commandments, especially in regard to loving Him and our fellow man, is the way to rid ourselves of such fear: "Whoever keeps His word, in him the love of God has truly been perfected. By this we know that we are in Him" (Col 3:14; 1 John 2:5-6; 4:8-18).

Again, YHVH wants to refine us, and in the process, because he loves us, He wants to speak to us—individually, face to face.

The Voice... Hearing the Almighty

Listen and Live

We are told that YHVH spoke to our forefathers with a "great/*gadol* voice."

His voice must have been an awesome sound that went right through the people. It must have made them feel like they would die if that voice of absolute truth continued to reverberate through their less-than-honest beings.

After hearing Him, Moses marveled at the idea and said, "We have seen today that our God speaks with man, yet he lives" (Deu 5:24).

It is possible for man to hear YHVH's great voice and live, but so often, like our forefathers, we tend to resist it.

So it is that now is the time for a paradigm shift in Israel's history. We need to change our view. It is time for all Israel to turn and go in the direction of that great voice. For, YHVH has sworn concerning those who resist Him: "...You shall perish; because you would not listen to the voice of YHVH your GOD" (Deu 8:20).

If we do not listen to Yah's great voice, we perish. When we do listen to His *gadol* voice, if there is any dross in us that He wants to burn out, His voice will burn very hot.

For this reason, we must ask our selves: Do we resist hearing His voice because we do not want to have our dross burned away? If so, now is the time to repent. Now is the time to ask the Father to speak to our hearts and to give us a spirit that is willing to obey and honor Him. Now is the time for all Israel to make *teshuvah*, meaning, to *repent* and *return* to the Holy One. [14]

---

[14] S&BDB word # H 7725. For more information regarding *Teshuvah*, see *Israel's Feasts and their Fullness: Expanded Edition*, Batya Ruth Wootten, Chapter 31, "Repentance and Returning – Tashlich and Teshuvah," 2008, Key of David Publishing, Saint Cloud, FL.

Forever Chosen to Choose

We began with three questions regarding the promise that, in the latter days Israel would return to YHVH and listen to His voice. Our questions were: to whom was the promise given, how should it affect their walk, and what does it mean to listen to YHVH's voice?

We now briefly address our first question: Who is supposed to return and begin to hear?

When Moses came down from the mountain after conversing with the Almighty, he presented an offer from the Holy One to all of the sons of Israel. It was an offer they could not refuse.

> "You yourselves have seen what I did to the Egyptians, and...now if you will indeed obey My voice and keep My covenant, then you shall be My own possession among all the peoples, for all the earth is Mine; and you shall be to Me a kingdom of priests and a holy nation" (Exo 19:4-6).

That was it. Israel was "forever 'chosen.'"

Because the Father loved their fathers, He *chose* their descendants after them (Deu 4:37). YHVH *chose, bachar, appointed,* [15] the sons of Israel when He said to them:

> "You are a holy people to YHVH your God; YHVH your God has chosen you to be a people for His own possession out of all the peoples on the face of the earth. YHVH did not set His love on you nor choose you because you were more in number than any of the peoples, for you were the fewest of all peoples, but because YHVH loved you and kept the oath which He swore to your forefathers....On your fathers did YHVH set His affection to love them, He chose their descendants after them, even you above all peoples as it is this day" (Deu 7:6-8; 10:15).

Because the children of Israel were *chosen,* in turn, they must make a *choice:* "I call heaven and earth to witness against you today, that I have set before you life and death, the blessing and the curse...so choose life in order that you may live, you and your descendants" (Deu 30:19).

Believe and Be Blessed
Doubt and Be Debased

If Israel will obey, they will be blessed. Their enemies will flee from before them. The Father will bless all that they put their hands to do. Thus all the people of the earth will know that the God of Israel indeed blesses His people (Deu 28:1-14).

On the other hand, if the sons of Israel refuse to obey, then curses will come upon and overtake them, and everyone will know that the God of Israel has a Law that He wants His people to honor. If they do not obey, curses, confusion, defeat and rebuke will reign in all they under-

---

[15] Bachar: *S&BDB* # H 977.

take to do, because they have forsaken the One who chose them. If they do not obey, they will be a scattered, miserable, wretched and accursed lot (Deu 28:15-68).

CHOSEN FOREVER

"You are My witnesses," the Father says of the children of Israel (Isa 43:10). Regardless of the path they choose, Israelite sheep are always being a witness, although their witness may be positive, negative, or a mix thereof. This is so because "the gifts and calling of God are without repentance" (Rom 11:29, KJV). All twelve tribes, whether they are aware of their heritage or are lost to it, have an "irrevocable call" on their lives. Our "God is not a man that He should lie...has He said, and will He not do it? Or has He spoken, and will He not make it good?" (Num 23:19). YHVH makes good on His promises. And He has chosen Israel's tribes forever. Israel is forever chosen to choose. The challenge that is forevermore before them is that of Joshua: *"Choose this day whom you will serve O Israel" (Josh 24:15).*

CHOSEN TO BE WITNESSES

The Father called all Israel to be His "witnesses." They were forever chosen to be a witness to the world that He alone is God. They were and are to proclaim to the world that He is the great "I AM" and that none can deliver out of His hand. They must tell the world that: Before Him there was no God formed and there will be none after Him. They must declare that there is no Savior besides Him. "Is there any God besides Me, or is there any other Rock? I know of none," says the Holy One of Israel (Isa 43:8-13; 44:8).

Israel has been forever called to be a witness for the God of Israel— which brings us to the issue of the identity of the One who called Israel to testify to the world about Him.

The Voice... Hearing the Almighty

To see Him for Who He is, and to better understand Israel, we first acknowledge that *YHVH Elohim* is the Inspiration behind the divine words of the Torah. He is the ultimate Author of Israel's Book of Covenants, both Old (First) and New (Renewed). Moreover, in those inspired Books He established an eternal Law in Israel— and it is an everlasting Law that He Himself must keep...

YHVH Must Have Two Witnesses

Our Father established the rule in Israel that, "two or more" must bear witness before a matter can be established, confirmed, and/or believed as being the truth (Num 35:30; Deu 17:6; 19:15). This principle of dual testimony is also upheld by both Messiah Yeshua and Paul the apostle: "It is written that the testimony of two persons is reliable and valid" (John 8:17). And, "Every matter must be established by the testimony of two or three witnesses" (2 Cor 13:1). We must understand this salient point of Biblical law, in Old Covenant and New, both the Father and Yeshua established the principle that, for a matter to be confirmed and/or believed in the Earth, it first must be upheld by "two or more witnesses." [16]

---

[16] This law reveals the plurality of the Almighty. He said, "No person shall be put to death on the testimony of one witness" (Num 35:30; Deu 19:15). He demands a plurality of witnesses to a crime before someone can be executed. "One" is here translated from *echad* and can mean a numeral, united, first, alike, alone, a man, only, other, together, same, single, each (*S&BDB* # H259; *TWOT* #61). *Echad* also is used to define our God in the *Shema*, the Deuteronomy 6:4 affirmation of faith: "Hear, O Israel... the LORD is one [*echad*]." *Echad* can mean alone, as in only, or it can mean together, as in one/united/same. As for human witnesses, *echad* must be taken in its "diversity within unity" meaning. Our God is to be the *One* and *Only* God of the Israelites – and His *echad* claim must be understood in its *plural form*. For, "Scripture cannot be broken" (John 10:35) and in it, YHVH is a witness against the children of Israel (Mal 3:5; Lev 20:5; Deu 32:35; Psa 96:13). If YHVH is singular, and has been a witness against a man that leads to his death, then He has broken Scripture. To be a Scripturally correct witness against man, He must be understood in the diversity within unity sense of *echad*. He is plural with
(continued...)

Forever Chosen To Choose

Yeshua said "Scripture cannot be broken" (John 10:35). So it is logical to conclude that they too must have confirming witnesses before their collective truth (Genesis to Revelation) can be established in the Earth.

Two Families — Chosen to Be Tested

Israel includes the "two families" whom the Father chose. They are His two *mishpachah*, His two *families*. [17] They also are called, His "two nations," and His two "kingdoms." *YHVH Tsava'ot*, the LORD of Hosts, calls them, "Both the houses of Israel." And, both houses— *and their companions*— are called to confirm the fullness of His truth in the earth (Isa 8:14; Jer 33:23-26; Eze 35:10; 37:15-28). Moreover, historically, Christians (Ephraim [18]) and Jews (Judah) have been the only two people groups in the earth who have acted as witnesses for *YHVH Elohim*.

Chosen Israel is also called to a *test*, because the word *chosen/bakar* also can be translated *tested*: "Behold, I have refined you, but not as silver; I have tested you in the furnace of affliction" (Isa 48:10). The *Theological Wordbook of the Old Testament*, says of the Hebrew word, *bachar*:

> "The root idea is evidently to 'take a keen look at' ...thus...the connotation of 'testing or examining' found in Isa 48:10....The word is used to express the choosing which has ultimate and eternal significance." [19]

To be *"chosen* Israel" means you will be *tested*. All Israel, *and their companions* are chosen: "You are a chosen race, a royal priesthood, a holy nation....you once were not a

---

16 (...continued)
Messiah Yeshua – who ultimately will be both Judge and Jury (John 1:1; 5:22-24,30-34; 12:48; Heb 4:12). (*Echad* idea by Judith Dennis.)

17 *S&BDB* # H 4940, a family, circle of relatives; a tribe, or people, kindred.

18 Gen 48:19; Hos 1-2; Rom 11.

19 *TWOT*, Moody Press, Chicago, 1985, # 231, Vol. I, p 100.

people, but now you are the people of God" (1 Pet 2:9-10). [20]

Blessing or curse? Which will we choose?

We cannot simply ignore the voice that calls from above. To do that is to choose the curse: "I brought you out of the land of Egypt, from the iron furnace, saying, 'Listen to My voice, and do according to all which I command you; so you shall be My people, and I will be your God.'" And, "I solemnly warn... even to this day... 'Listen to My voice.'"

Samuel said, "Has YHVH as much delight in burnt offerings and sacrifices as in obeying the voice of YHVH? Behold, to obey is better than sacrifice, and to heed than the fat of rams" (Jer 11:4,7; 1 Sam 15:22).

Like a child we must learn to obey the Father, even when we do not fully understand what He is asking of us (Pro 3:5). We obey because we know that He is our *Abba*. Messiah Yeshua taught us to pray, "Our Father [Abba] who is in heaven, Hallowed be Your name..." (Mat 6:9). We must know our Creator, not only as our "Lord" (or Master), but we must trust that He is our Father, our *Daddy*. We must have faith in Him and His love for us. For, "Without faith it is impossible to please Him." We must believe that "He is a rewarder of those who seek Him" (Heb 11:6).

We also must realize that, in the Garden, we chose not to obey, but to instead eat of the Tree of Knowledge of Good and Evil, and we have been having to choose between the two ever since. For this reason, we need to choose to follow the Spirit, and not our carnal minds. [21]

So it is that, in our day, the eternal call to choose continues to be upon both houses— Judah and Ephraim.

Shema Yisrael... Hear, understand, and obey, O Israel.
Choose this day whom you will serve (Josh 24:15).
Set your face this day O Israel to pass YHVH's test.

---

[20] Vessels of mercy: See Jer 31:20; Hos 1-2; Rom 9:16-20.
[21] See *Israel– Empowered by the Spirit*, by Smith and Wootten, chapter 3, "Burying Our Sinful Nature," 2009, Key of David Publishing, Saint Cloud, FL.

A Recap: Who Should Hear?

The Holy One said to the children of Israel who had been wandering in the wilderness, "In the latter days you will return to YHVH your God and listen to His voice" (Deu 4:30). When last-days Israel becomes *repentant* and makes *teshuvah*, they will listen to the voice of the Holy One. They will return and be obedient to Him alone.

Surely we are presently closer in time to the latter days than any generation that has gone before us. So now must be the time for Israel to heed the call to listen to the Father's voice. Now is the time for us to realize that, when Abba spoke of Israel returning and having a changed heart, He spoke of all twelve tribes of Israel. He did not speak of the Jewish people alone, but of *all Israel*, of both houses, Ephraim and Judah.

Even so, both houses now need to repent of their particular sins and begin to truly listen to the Holy One.

The Voice... Hearing the Almighty

Most Believers in the Messiah agree that, in the last days, the Holy One is dealing with "Israel." Thus it is imperative that we understand the identity of *all* Israel if we are to understand the importance of accurately hearing Abba's voice at this time— because this prophesied last-days' hearing has everything to do with the restoration of both the houses of Israel.

As was prophesied, "both the houses of Israel" have stumbled over the One who would be a Sanctuary to them (Isa 8:13-14; John 2:19-22). Both Judah and Ephraim have stumbled over Messiah Yeshua. He is denied in Judaism and misrepresented in Christianity. And, now is the time to seek the truth, as well as our full restoration. [22] As for our restoration, we note a promise in Isaiah: "They also that erred in spirit shall come to understanding, and they that murmured shall learn doctrine" (Isa 29:24).

We have definitely labored under the burden of unsound doctrine when it comes to all Israel and her Messiah. We also have erred in "spirit" with our mistaken understandings of the Ruach haKodesh.

To gain full impact of the meaning of the above Isaiah verse, we note that rebels murmur, and rebellion is said to be as the sin of witchcraft. Moreover, stubbornness is likened to iniquity and idolatry (Num 17:10; 1 Sam 15:23).

In many ways we stand guilty of these serious sins.

This is not said to condemn but to encourage. For the truth is, because we are willing to "rebel," we have dared to stand up for what is right. But as is often so, our greatest gift can become our downfall. In the past, we have stood against error, but we must not let fearlessness go too far. We must not be rebellious. It is now time for us to repent of our resistance toward the Holy Spirit and to allow Him to lead and guide us into sound scriptural doctrine.

---

[22] Both Houses: See Gen 48:19; Isa 8:14; Eze 37:15-28; Rom 11:25. Ephraim's Return: See Hos 1:10; 5:15; 6:1; 12:6; 14:2.

A Recap: Who Should Hear?

A Cleansed, Whole Israel

Scripture speaks of a special, anointed time when the two houses unite:

> "'The sons of Israel will come, both they and the sons of Judah as well; they will go along weeping as they go, and it will be YHVH their God they will seek. They will ask for the way to Zion, turning their faces in its direction; they will come that they may join themselves to YHVH in an everlasting covenant....At that time...search will be made for the iniquity of Israel, but there will be none; and for the sins of Judah, but they will not be found'" (Jer 50:4-5,20).
>
> Those once called "faithless Israel and treacherous Judah" will yet return to Zion. YHVH will give them shepherds who are after His heart. And "they will call Jerusalem, the Throne of YHVH...[and] will not walk anymore after the stubbornness of their evil heart. In those days the house of Judah will walk with the house of Israel" (Jer 3:14-18).

Abba wants both the houses of Israel— *and their companions*— to be reunited, to become one people, one stick in His hand. That reunited people is ultimately destined to walk in sinlessness. They will have YHVH's eternal Law written on their hearts by the Holy Spirit (Heb 8:8).

With this restoration, the Holy One will plant His chosen people in His land (Eze 37:16; Isa 56:3-6). Then, they will no more defile themselves with *any* of their transgressions. In the end, this promise, this high call, will include *all* who are part of the commonwealth of Israel (Eph 2:11-22). It ultimately will include all who follow Israel's Messiah.

Yet, some claim this work of restoration is something the Messiah alone will do when He returns to Earth.

The Voice... Hearing the Almighty

This attitude, too, is in error. YHVH put Adam and Eve in the Garden and told them to "keep it." He uses His people, empowered by His Spirit, to accomplish His work in the earth. The same will be true of Israel's restoration. But, even if it were true that Messiah will one day "do all the work," His eternal plan must still be written on our hearts. At the very least, we should be praying, on a daily basis, even as He instructed us to pray: "'*Your kingdom come. Your will be done, on earth* as it is in heaven" (Mat 6:10).

We initially asked the questions, to whom was the promise given, and how should it affect their walk?

The answers are that, *we are part of the people of Israel— and our Messiah wants to use us to help restore His kingdom!*

Having established these points, we now pursue answers to the questions, what does it mean to hear the Spirit? How do we learn to hear the voice of the Holy One? And, as New Covenant Believers, what *Law* is it that *we* are to obey?

Thus Far...

We have thus far seen the following:

- In the latter days Israel's scattered tribes, and their companions, return to the Holy One
- When they do, they will hear and obey His voice
- The Father tests all of chosen Israel, to see if they will obey and follow Him
- After the original sin, Adam and Eve heard the Creator's voice outside themselves
- Our New Covenant sojourn on earth is about our being restored to the Father's Spirit guidance, about getting His voice back inside us
- There are two houses of Israel and both are being called to reunite and return to the Holy One, and to, at last, learn to listen to and obey His voice.

SEVEN

THE ESSENCE OF THE NEW COVENANT

Realizing that the voice of the Holy One was outside man after his fall helps us see the New Covenant in a different light. We gain new insight as to its purpose and thrust. We see that Messiah Yeshua's New Covenant is about redeeming us from our sin and about restoring the Father's Spirit guidance to our internal beings. It is about our learning to hear and being obedient to His voice as we develop an intimate relationship with Him:

> "'Behold, days are coming...when I will make a new covenant with the house of Israel and with the house of Judah, not like the covenant which I made with their fathers in the day I took them by the hand to bring them out of the land of Egypt, My covenant which they broke, although I was a husband to them... But this is the covenant which I will make with the

house of Israel after those days...I will put My law within them and on their heart I will write it; and I will be their God, and they shall be My people. They will not teach again, each man his neighbor and each man his brother, saying, "Know YHVH," for they will all know Me, from the least of them to the greatest of them...for I will forgive their iniquity, and their sin I will remember no more'" (Jer 31:31-34).

Yeshua's New Covenant

Yeshua instituted this promised New Covenant with the sons of Israel who were seated around His Passover table. He said, "This cup is the new covenant in my blood, which is poured out for you" (Luke 22:20, NIV). [23]

We enter into this New Covenant through faith in our Redeemer, Messiah Yeshua. And He said, "The Counselor, the Holy Spirit, whom the Father will send in my name, will teach you all things and will remind you of everything I have said to you" (John 14:26). Yeshua established the New Covenant, but He left its implementation up to the Holy Spirit.

We see the role of the Spirit in the New Covenant in that, when He fell on those of the nations who were listening to Peter's message, it served as a sign to the apostles that those on whom He had fallen were to be accepted into Israel's commonwealth. In other words, exhibiting evidence that the Holy Spirit was active in their lives, that they were *hearing Him*, gave testimony that they too had entered into Israel's New Covenant. We might say, having the Spirit fall on them marked them as children who belonged to the God of Israel (Acts 10:44-48; Eph 2:11-22).

Selah. Let us once again pause and meditate.

---

[23] Also see Heb 8:6-12; 1 Cor 5:7; 11:25; *Israel's Feasts and their Fullness: Expanded Edition*, Batya Ruth Wootten, Passover Section.

EIGHT

THE SHEEN AND THE SPIRIT

Most Believers agree that the Father gave the Ten Commandments to the children of Israel on the feast of Shavuot (Pentecost), and that on a Shavuot day many years later, the Ruach haKodesh was poured out on Yeshua's disciples as they were gathered together in prayer (Exo 19:9-25; 20:1-21; Acts 2:1-4).

John the Baptist said he baptized people in water for repentance, but that, the Messiah would baptize them "with the Holy Spirit and *fire*" (Luke 3:16).

When Yeshua's disciples were baptized in the Spirit and began to speak in other tongues, they saw tongues as of fire over their heads: "There appeared unto them *cloven* tongues like as of fire, and it sat upon each of them. And they were all filled with the Holy Spirit, and began to speak with other tongues, as the Spirit gave them utterance" (Acts 2:3-4, KJV).

Exactly what is it that appeared over their heads?

It was surely a sign from above— but what did it mean?

Cloven Tongues of Fire

Fire represents our God. He is a consuming fire who speaks from the midst of the fire, thus showing His greatness. He goes before us as a consuming pillar of fire and defeats our enemies with a word. When Moses was with YHVH on Mount Horeb, He "wrote on the tablets the words of the covenant, the Ten Commandments [Ten Words]." In the "midst of fire" He wrote them. [24]

With the New Covenant outpouring of the Spirit, the Law that was once written on tablets of stone by the fiery finger of God began to be written with fire on hearts of flesh by the Spirit of God. [25]

Fire purifies. The trials and fires of life forge spiritual character. When we follow the Lamb of God, we are tested, purified by, and baptized with His fire. Even so, our God warns, "Those whom the LORD loves He disciplines, and He scourges every son whom He receives" (Zec 13:9). Because He loves us, He sends His cleansing fire. [26]

Concerning this Shavuot outpouring, the King James refers to its fire as "cloven tongues." The NIV describes it as "tongues of fire that *separated*." The word in question is *diamerizo*, which means to partition, divide, or part. [27]

What kind of fire was the Messiah putting on His people?

While the theory cannot be proven, there is an interesting explanation as to what the disciples might have actually seen....

---

[24] Exo 13:21; 34:28; Deu 4:24,33; 5:24-26; 9:10;10:4,13. Words: *S&BDB* # H1697. The Ten Words are His "Covenant" (Deu 4:13); and these Commandments/Laws will be in effect forever.

[25] Israel came to Mount Sinai on the third day of the third month, Yah visited the people three days later (Exo 19:1,10-17). This is thought to have happened 50 days after they crossed the Red Sea, on the day that came to be known as the feast of Shavuot. Exo 19:9-20:21; Jer 31:31-33; Acts 2:1-4; 2 Cor 3:3; Heb 8:8-13; 10:16-17.

[26] Mat 3:11; Luke 3:16; James 1:12; 1 Pet 1:7; Heb 12:6; Rev 3:18.

[27] *Strong's* # G1266; to partition thoroughly: cloven, divide, part.

The Sheen and the Spirit

A day is coming when Believers, like the High Priests of old, will have the Father's name "written on their foreheads" (Exo 28:38; Rev 7:2-4; 14:1; 22:4). Could the cloven tongues of fire represent a similar mark? Could it even represent the *initial* of the Almighty? In Hebrew, God Almighty is *El Shaddai*. He is known in Jewish circles by this name, and the first Hebrew letter in the name *Shaddai* (Almighty), is *sheen* (שׁ). This letter is likened in Hebraic thought to His *initial* and is often used to represent Him.

The Sheen and the Ruach

The name, *El Shaddai*, means "The Power," or "The God that cannot be obstructed." Thus the common translation, the *Almighty*. In Hebrew, *Shaddai* is written with the letters, *sheen, dalet, yod*. We see the first letter, sheen, in the box at right, marked "Hebrew Sheen." Below it, we see a stylized "Flaming Sheen." Finally, we see a "Disciple" with what might appear to Hebrew people as a *flaming sheen*, a sign that the Almighty is putting His mark, His *initial*, on His chosen people.

Whether this is true or not, we do know that on a Shavuot day long ago, the disciples gathered in the Upper Room had "cloven tongues of fire" fall on them. *El Shaddai* poured out His Spirit on them and they were forever changed. Divinely marked, they were thereafter empowered by the Holy One of Israel. We who love the God of Israel and follow His Messiah, should, of all people, be so marked. Like Peter and the disciples of old, we too need to have the same life-changing power fall on us.

Hebrew Sheen

Flaming Sheen

Disciple receiving the mark of the Sheen— the mark of the Holy Spirit

EMPOWERED FROM ON HIGH

Earlier, Messiah Yeshua told His disciples, "Behold, I am sending forth the promise of My Father upon you; but you are to stay in the city until you are *clothed/endued/arrayed* with power from on high" (Luke 24:49).

The word translated *endued* is from the Greek, *enduo*, and means to sink into a garment, to invest with clothing, to endow with a quality or ability, to array, clothe, endue with, to have, or put on power. [28]

We know the feast of Passover was fulfilled by Messiah Yeshua, and that, after Passover, comes the feast of Shavuot. We especially need to rediscover this feast, because in it, we are empowered to walk in the days to come. It depicts us being clothed with the power necessary to walk toward the days of the Fall Feasts, which symbolize the return of our Messiah.

NAKED AND KNOWING

YHVH has always been concerned with how we are dressed. In the Garden, Adam and Eve feared because they ate from the tree of the knowledge of good and evil and then saw their *nakedness*. So, "YHVH made garments of skin for Adam and his wife, and clothed them" (Gen 3:21). This depicts the truth that our sin must be covered.

However, we again note that Adam realized and confessed that he was "naked" (Gen 3:10-11). The Hebrew word used here, *ay-rome*, is rooted in the word *arum*, which is used in Genesis 3:1 to describe *the Accuser, haSatan:* "Now the serpent was more crafty than any beast of the field which the LORD God had made. And he said to the woman, 'Indeed, has God said, "You shall not eat from any tree of the garden"?'"

---

[28] *Strong's* # G1746.

Ay-rome (naked) is variously translated as *subtle, shrewd,* and *crafty.* In this way we see that Adam's nakedness had more to do with his actions than the state of his body. [29]

This idea is affirmed in that YHVH Elohim said of him, "Behold, the man has become like one of Us, *knowing* good and evil..." (Gen 3:22). It is in thinking we *know,* and not listening to the voice of the Holy One, that we go astray. We thus become *cunning*, like the one who deceived us. Nonetheless, Father God, in His mercy, clothes us with animal skins. This action depicts the truth that a sacrifice will have to be made for us, something will have to die in our place— so our sin can be "covered." The perfect Sacrifice is found in Messiah Yeshua. We thus look to Him to clothe us in true righteousness. We want to cease being cunning and instead learn to walk in true righteousness.

When Adam sinned, the Father asked him two questions: *"Where are you?"* And, *"Who told you that you were naked?"* YHVH is all knowing and did not need to get inforation from mortal Adam. His rhetorical questions were asked in hopes of getting Adam to examine his self. We too need to examine ourselves (2 Cor 13:5). We want to ask of our self, *"Where am I? Who told me the things I am basing my life on?"* And, *"Am I truly listening to the Father's voice?"*

Properly Dressed Priests

YHVH said He would clothe the priests of Zion with salvation (Psa 132:13-16). The meaning of Yeshua's name is "Salvation," and we are to be clothed in Him. Similarly, the clothing of the High Priest included a breast plate with twelve stones on it, one for each of Israel's tribes. This shows us that, if we are going to be priests who minister to YHVH, we must love and care about all twelve tribes. Their unified presence must always be on our hearts.

---

29 *S&BDB* word #'s H 5903; 6191.

Dressed as the Bride —
And as the Bridegroom

Isaiah said, "I will rejoice greatly in YHVH, my soul will exult in my God; for He has clothed me with garments of salvation, He has wrapped me with a robe of righteousness, as a bridegroom decks himself with a garland, and as a bride adorns herself with her jewels" (Isa 61:10).

Here we see that we are to be dressed as both a bridegroom *and* a bride.

When we see ourselves as the bride of Messiah, we realize that we are to keep ourselves pure and chaste for Him. However, as members of *His Body*, we also are typified as being part of the *Bridegroom*. Even so, Isaiah reveals that *Jerusalem* is the bride. And, bridegrooms traditionally care for and protect their bride— which is why we are called to pray, care for, and protect New Jerusalem (Psa 122:6; Isa 54:5; 62:1-6; Eph 1:22-23; Col 1:24; Rev 21:2).

When we are baptized into Messiah, we are clothed with Messiah. We buy from Him, without cost, white garments to cover our nakedness. We are to walk with Him dressed in white robes, clothed in fine linen, bright and clean. That "fine linen is...the righteous acts of the saints" (Gal 3:27; Rev 3:4,18; 7:9; 19:8,14).

Asking the Helper to Dress Us

While in this earth, how can we know if we are appropriately dressed and truly clothed in Messiah's righteousness?

In Esther 1-2 we see that "when the turn came for Esther... to go to the king, she asked for nothing other than what Hegai, the king's eunuch...suggested. And Esther won the favor of everyone who saw her" (Esther 2:14-15).

The Sheen and the Spirit

The Holy Spirit is said to be our "Helper," and, like the eunuch who knew and helped the king, so the Holy Spirit knows what pleases King Messiah. Again, Yeshua said, "Stay in the city until you are *clothed/endued/arrayed with power from on high*" (John 14:16, 26; 15:26; 16:7; Luke 24:49).

The Ruach haKodesh must be the one to dress us. If we want to please our King, if we want to be His Bride, if we want to see all Israel restored, we must allow the Holy Spirit to clothe and empower us.

When the Holy Spirit does clothe us, He does so from the inside out. He first deals with matters of the heart. Being marked with the fire of the Holy Spirit gives evidence that we are being clothed/empowered from on High. YHVH begins to clothe our *spirit man* with His righteousness.

Israel has a history of resisting the Ruach, but YHVH said, "Circumcise your heart, and stiffen your neck no longer" (Deu 10:16). In Acts 7:51, Stephen said, "You men who are stiff-necked and uncircumcised in heart and ears are always resisting the Holy Spirit; you are doing just as your fathers did."

If we want to see Israel's dry bones come to life, we must first begin to walk according to Ezekiel 36:27: "I will put My Spirit within you and cause you to walk in My statutes, and you will be careful to observe My ordinances."

If we want to see the two sticks of Ezekiel reunited and restored, we first must embrace the truth of Ezekiel 37:14: "I will put My Spirit within you and you will come to life, and I will place you on your own land. Then you will know that I, YHVH, have spoken and done it."

If we want to see fulfillment of all of the Father's latter-day prophetic promises, we must first believe Ezekiel 39:29: "I will not hide My face from them any longer, for I will have poured out My Spirit on the house of Israel,' declares YHVH Elohim."

We also must believe Joel 2:28-29: "It will come about after this that I will pour out My Spirit on all mankind; and your sons and daughters will prophesy, your old men will dream dreams, your young men will see visions. Even on the male and female servants I will pour out My Spirit in those days."

> *Israel, we must receive the Spirit!*
> *We must allow Him to clothe us from on High!*
> *We cannot be what we are called to be apart from Yah's promised empowerment by the Ruach haKodesh!*

Last Days Dangers

Our Messiah promised to give to those who ask, a spiritual well of living water. He said He would guide us to springs of the water of life and give to the one who thirsts from the spring of the water of life without cost (John 4:10,14; 7:37-39; Rev 7:17; 21:6).

In Revelation 22:1-2 we see that an angel showed John this river of the water of life, clear as crystal, coming from the throne of God and of the Lamb. On either side was the tree of life, bearing twelve kinds of fruit. In verse 22:17 we read, "The Spirit and the bride say, 'Come.' Let the one who hears say, 'Come.' Let the one who is thirsty come; let the one who wishes take the water of life without cost."

We are promised an unending supply of living water, an abundant River of Life. But, in this life Israel must beware, because in the last days, Satan pours out of his mouth a River of Death. His dangerous deluge is sent to sweep us away: "And the serpent poured water like a river out of his mouth after the woman, so that he might cause her to be swept away with the flood" (Rev 12:15).

Words come out of the mouth. And in these last days, the Accuser of the Brethren, *haSatan*, is sending forth from his mouth a flood of words. Moreover, the stated purpose of these words is to sweep away the woman, Israel.

The Serpent spewed forth deceptive words in *Gan Eden*. With them, deceived Eve was swept away, along with compromising Adam. Satan continues to use his same old method of deception. In the Garden he distorted Abba's Word, and he continues to twist Abba's truth in our day.

How is this end-time prophecy being fulfilled?

In our day we see a flood of information on the Internet. We also see an unhealthy reverence for "knowledge" in our movement. In the early church, love of head knowledge, love of "knowing," was called *Gnosticism*. We now see a rebirth of this age-old sin. In our ranks we see a lust for, even a worship of, head knowledge. And, because she does not "know" certain things, the Church is disparaged, and all things related to her are thrown out the window. She is like the proverbial baby that gets thrown out with the dirty bath water.

While we must rid ourselves of Church errors, we must keep some essential and foundational truths she has been used to bring forth to the world, such as the fact that the Creator has an Only Begotten Son Who paid the price for our sins and that He loves us and wants to restore us. [30]

In short, if we want the truth, we must have the Spirit, because "The Spirit is the truth" (1 John 5:6). So it is that we desperately need to bring balance to our movement— and we can best do that by opening up our hearts to the voice of the Holy Spirit. [31]

Abba, please fill our bellies now with the promised Living Water of Your Holy Spirit (John 7:37-39).

---

[30] When we repent, Messiah cleanses us and gives us new life in Him; in which we are to walk as He walked, in righteousness. Through faith in Him we are cleansed, then seek to walk in His Way (Acts 24:14; James 2:14-22; 1 John 1:7; 2:6).

[31] Voice of the Spirit: I.E., see Acts 4:8; 8:29; 10:19; 13:2.

TEN

The Idolatry of Intellect

The following message was delivered by Hale Harris, General Secretary of the Messianic Israel Alliance. At an MIA Conference, Hale addressed the problems that arise from putting excessive emphasis on human knowledge and reasoning—and not allowing room for the Holy Spirit to speak to us. Hale begins:

> "We should take care not to make the intellect our god; it has, of course, powerful muscles, but no personality."
> - Albert Einstein

When Adam and Eve were in the Garden of Eden they enjoyed fellowship with their Creator. The Garden was a place of beauty, order, and intimacy.

Adam was told to cultivate and keep the Garden. We might say that Adam's charge was to guard this place of intimacy between man and God.

In the Garden, Yahweh walked in the cool of the evening (Gen 3:8). We can assume that Adam and Eve were free to walk with Him, rejoicing in their position as children of God, asking their Father questions, and simply delighting in His presence.

Adam was more than able to take care of this beautiful garden as long as fellowship with God was intact. Adam received instruction and wisdom from His Father on a daily basis. Kingdom order was quite simple. If Adam obeyed God things would continue to go well: "From any tree of the garden you may eat freely," He was told, "but from the tree of the knowledge of good and evil you shall not eat, for in the day that you eat from it you will surely die" (Gen 2:17).

We are all familiar with the sad turn of events. Through Adam's disobedience, sin entered the world and "death through sin" (Rom 5:12). The law of sin and death then became reality on planet Earth. Adam and Eve were driven from the Garden and from Yahweh's presence.

When Adam chose to disobey God he was, in essence, exalting his own intellect above his Creator's. He adopted the attitude that he knew better than God. Through his choice, Adam removed God as the supreme authority in his life and made his own intellect master instead. By exalting himself, Adam was humbled, and the result was the curse.

In God's plan of redemption, the solution to this rebellion is found in the last Adam. Yeshua came and did only what the Father told Him to do. He spoke only the words the Father told Him to speak (John 6:38-40; 12:49). Unlike the first Adam, Yeshua humbled himself so that He, and all who abide in Him, might be exalted (see Luke 14:11; 1 Cor 15:45). Yeshua came to reestablish correct Kingdom order through the Holy Spirit.

The *Ruach haKodesh* is truly the implantation of God's life in us. When the Spirit indwells a person, it is now possible to once again experience that intimacy and fellowship, which is the essence of worship (John 4:24). It is now possible to receive instruction directly from the Father—

what some call revelation. [32] One of the names of the Holy Spirit is the "Spirit of Truth"(John 15:26; 16:13). A good definition for truth is "ultimate reality." The Spirit leads us to walk in ultimate reality. This is the way things really are, whether seen or unseen.

But as wonderful as the ministry of the Holy Spirit is, the intellect of man is reluctant to relinquish the throne. We want to run the show. We want to figure everything out. We want everything to make sense according to human logic and deductive reasoning.

This is why the gifts of the Holy Spirit are such a subject of contention. They are not of this world. They operate apart from natural understanding. They transcend the bounds of human thought and undermine the supremacy of human intellect. This unnerves some of us. So in order to keep intellect in its comfortable position of power, we analyze every move of the Spirit. If we allow the gifts to operate at all, we keep them on a tight, intellectual leash. Then we wonder why miracles, signs, and wonders aren't taking place in our midst.

Meanwhile, overseas, "primitive" cultures are experiencing the power of God on a level like that of the early Messianic community: The blind see and the lame walk. People are raised from the dead. We hear these reports but we know these people don't know what we know. Their theology is not as accurate as ours. So we filter the reports through our superior western intellect and dismiss them.

Please don't misinterpret what I'm saying. I am not anti-intellectual. C.S. Lewis wrote that "God is no fonder of intellectual slackers than any other slackers."

Yahweh gave us a mind and we should develop and use it to the best of our ability. And I do believe there is such a thing as being so open minded your brains can fall

---

[32] The word "revelation" is used in the sense of specific, supernatural information given by God, not in the general sense of anything that is discovered or revealed.

out. But we must understand that our minds were created to be in subjection to our spirits and to the Father of Spirits (Heb 12:9). We might say we are to be ruled from the inside out, and the spirit is our innermost being (John 7:38). True living water flows from the innermost being, not from anywhere else.

Rabbi *Shaul* [the Apostle Paul] wrote, "Now we have received, not the spirit of the world, but the Spirit who is from God, so that we may know the things freely given to us by God, which things we also speak, not in words taught by human wisdom, but in those taught by the Spirit, combining spiritual thoughts with spiritual words" (1 Cor 2:12-13). Our intellect, powerful though it may be, has been programmed by the enemy and fallen creation. It makes a poor ruler. It must be restored in proper relationship to the Father's superior understanding via the Holy Spirit. It must be renewed (Rom 12:2). In Isaiah we read, "'My thoughts are not your thoughts, nor are your ways My ways,' declares the LORD. 'For as the heavens are higher than the earth, so are My ways higher than your ways and My thoughts than your thoughts'" (Isa 55:8-9).

The idol of intellectualism is sometimes manifested within the body of believers by those whom I call "knowledge brokers." I don't mean to be hyper-critical in saying this, but these are people with teaching gifts who are full of information and scholarly knowledge. Certainly, we need gifted teachers who unlock the meaning of the scriptures and illuminate the plan of God. But some have determined that the success of their ministry depends upon impressing people with the latest, most-profound, cutting-edge teaching. They feel pressure to push the envelope and deliver a message that will impress and astound. After all, it's a competitive world out there. So, week after week, they amaze us with information and pummel us with profundity.

THE IDOLATRY OF INTELLECT

Yet, their teaching is not making many true disciples of Yeshua. In fact, at the end of the day, people seem to be more excited about the knowledge broker than they do about the God he represents.

Meanwhile, our neighbor is dying of cancer, our best friend is getting a divorce, and our nephew is on drugs. And we haven't been equipped to help them. We do have, however, a head full of information.

Yahweh said in Exodus 19, "You yourselves have seen what I did to the Egyptians, and how I bore you on eagles' wings, and brought you to Myself" (vs. 4). Let's not miss the message of that simple statement. We were delivered from bondage in order to be brought to a person, and that person is our Heavenly Father. Our earthly sojourn is not just about gathering information about Him— it is instead about our meeting with Him, worshiping Him, serving Him, and loving Him. We must come to our Father every day and spend time with Him in prayer and praise. He will speak to us when we do.

As God's children, we are to be like our Father. *Shaul* (Paul) instructed us in Philippians 2 to be "like-minded, having the same love, being of one accord, of one mind. Let this mind be in you, which was also in Messiah Yeshua. He humbled Himself, and became obedient unto death, even the death of the cross."

As we humble ourselves and seek our Father's thoughts above our own ideas, bringing into captivity every thought to the obedience of Messiah (2 Cor 10:5)— He'll give us the anointing and revelation we need.

Einstein was right:
Take care not to make the intellect your god. [33]

---

[33] *The Idolatry of Intellect*, by Hale Harris, General Secretary, Messianic Israel Alliance: www.messianicisrael.com/newsroom.
Reprinted with permission.

The Voice... Hearing the Almighty

Lawlessness and a Renewed Commandment

Eleven

Two potential pitfalls await last-days Israel. They are legalism and lawlessness.

Legalism is a killer. It is rooted in following the "letter of the Law," and it brings death. Legalism kills the spirit of those who promote it, and it turns away many who might otherwise be drawn to the Messiah and His truths. [34]

The human mind can focus only on one thing at a time. Focusing on the letter of the Law and in particular, on how others may or may not be "obeying" those Laws, takes our focus off our self. It then possibly becomes for us even as Messiah once asked of a man: "Why do you look at the speck that is in your brother's eye, but do not notice the log that is in your own eye?"

---

[34] Rom 2:27; 7:6; 8:2-4; Gal 3:2-5; 5:18.

Yeshua further asked of this man, "How can you say to your brother, 'Brother, let me take out the speck that is in your eye,' when you yourself do not see the log that is in your own eye? You hypocrite, first take the log out of your own eye, and then you will see clearly to take out the speck that is in your brother's eye" (Luke 6:41-42).

When we have a log of legalism in our own eye, we cannot see well enough to help our brother.

To preach true Torah, we must first examine our heart and ask Abba to reveal to us the truth of what lies there. Then we will be better equipped to share Torah— but for the purpose of nourishing and strengthening the hearer. [35]

Harsh judgment awaits all hypocrites and we do not want to be counted among them. We instead want to walk as Messiah walked. He comes to us in love, and, "The one who says he abides in Him ought himself to walk in the same manner as He walked" (1 John 2:6).

We do not want to be legalistic. Yeshua had harsh words for those who fell into that trap: "Woe to you, teachers of the law and Pharisees, you hypocrites! You travel over land and sea to win a single convert, and when he becomes one, you make him twice as much a son of hell as you are" (Mat 23:15).

On the other hand, neither do we want to be regarded by our Messiah as having been "lawless." To be lawless is to be unregulated, ungoverned, without, or not in conformity with, the Law. Yeshua warned that one day, He would say of such people:

> "Not everyone who says to me, 'Lord, Lord,' shall enter the kingdom of heaven, but he who does the will of my Father in heaven. Many will say to me in that day, 'Lord, Lord, have we not prophesied in your name, cast out demons in your name, and done many

---

[35] See *Mama's Torah: The Role of Women* by Batya Ruth Wootten, 2004: Key of David Publishing. Saint Cloud, FL.

wonders in your name?' Then I will declare to them, I never knew you; depart from me, you who practice lawlessness!" (Mat 7:21-23, NKJV).

These people will be rejected because they are *evildoers, workers of iniquity,* and *lawless ones.* Yeshua will tell them to "Depart" from Him (Mat 7:23; Luke 13:27).

Iniquity speaks of *injustice,* unrighteousness. Lawlessness, or *anomia,* means violation of law, wickedness, and transgression. *Anomia* is from *anomos,* and speaks of those who do not subject themselves to the Law. By implication they are thus a heathen Gentile— meaning someone that is not counted among the chosen, separated, covenant-keeping people of Israel. [36]

"Lawlessness" is a "mystery" that is "now at work in the earth." It consists of deliberate, persistent sin, of willful refusal to admit to and turn from evil. It is disobedience, a spiritual rebellion that takes deep root; it is deluding and even dismisses charges of wrong-doing. Lawlessness is an internal sin that ultimately produces the external fruit of transgression (2 Th 2:7; Heb 3:10-12).

Those who are guilty of this sin can sometimes work signs, wonders, and miracles. But in the end, it gains them nothing. Yeshua refuses them entry into His Kingdom.

These people are counted out because they refused to recognize and obey the eternal truth of YHVH's Ten Commandments; they do not realize that they are His Covenant. Moses said, "He declared to you His covenant which He commanded you to perform, that is, the Ten Commandments; and He wrote them on two tablets of stone." His Covenant Tablets were carried by the Levites in the "Ark of the Covenant." We must not reject *any* of His Ten Commandments if we want to be counted among His covenant people (Deu 4:13; 31:9).

---

[36] See, *Strong's,* Workers, #G2040. Iniquity, #G93. Lawlessness/anomia, #'s G458 and 459, respectively. Gentiles, # G 1482.

Some teach lawlessness to their own ruin and encourage others to do the same. Such deceived ones are said to be *many* and they are able to work *miracles* in the Master's Name (Mat 7:21-23). Still, He rejects them. [37]

We therefore should ask, *what voice were they listening to?*

Surely it was not that of the Holy One. And surely, we do not want to perish with them. We do not want to be included in their devastating dismissal. Yet, we must agree that the Church is right in that, the Law of the Spirit of life in Messiah Yeshua has set us free from the law of sin and of death. In Him, we are made servants of a new covenant, not of the letter but of the Spirit; for the letter kills, but the Spirit gives life (Rom 7:4; 8:2; 2 Cor 3:6).

The Law of the Spirit is to be written on our hearts by the Spirit. [38] Hebrews 8:8-12 affirms Jeremiah's promise that, when the New Covenant is in *full* effect, we will all know our God and that He will have written His Law on our hearts. Thus, we need to know what that Law is, as well as how we can avoid breaking it.

To identify this Law, and to keep us from the pitfall of lawlessness, we note that Messiah Yeshua said, "A *new* commandment I give to you, that you love one another, even as I have loved you, that you also love one another" (John 13:34).

Often called the "Law of Love," many have taught that Messiah's "Love Commandment" was "new," and that it supersedes all Old Covenant commandments.

However, the Greek word here translated *new*, is rooted in a word that also can mean *renew* or *regenerate*. [39] If we view Messiah's statement in light of verses from the apostle John, we see that the word "renewed" is a better fit.

---

[37] See *Israel– Empowered by the Spirit*, by Wallace E. Smith and Batya Ruth Wootten, chapter 2, "Counterfeits and Disobedience," 2009, Key of David Publishing, Saint Cloud, FL.
[38] Jer 31:31; Luke 22:20; 1 Cor 11:25; Heb 8:,13; 9:15; 12:24.
[39] *Strong's* #'s G2537; 3501.

LAWLESSNESS AND A RENEWED COMMANDMENT

John writes, "Beloved, I am *not* writing a new commandment to you, but an old commandment which you have had from the beginning....[It is] not as though I were writing to you a new commandment, but the one which we have had from the beginning, that we love one another. And this is love, that we walk according to His commandments. This is the commandment, just as you have heard from the beginning, that you should walk in it" (1 John 2:7-8; 2 John 1:5-6).

John is right. The command to love was given to ancient Israel. YHVH repeatedly said we were to love Him with all our heart, soul, and might, and love our neighbor as ourselves. [40] The call to love is as foundational to our faith as is Torah and the Ten Commandments. We were taught to love from the beginning, and it is not wise to use this verse to dismiss Messiah's instructions to us. For He said, "If you love Me, *keep My commandments*" (John 14:15-24).

Messiah summed up the Torah in two Commandments: *Love* the LORD and *love* your neighbor. [41] James said, "If, you are fulfilling the royal law according to the Scripture, 'You shall *love* your neighbor as yourself,' you are doing well" (James 2:8).

The "if" attached to James' statement has to do with love's being defined "according to the Scripture." He surely had the ancient verses in mind in saying this. They were the standard by which Israel measured love of God and neighbor. So, it is foolish for us to dismiss Torah's eternal wisdom. YHVH says of His commandments, "Keep and do them, for that is your wisdom and your understanding in the sight of the peoples." We keep them so we will be made strong enough to possess His land (Deu 4:6; 5:29; 11:8). Dismissing His essential standards leads to lawlessness, and ultimately to our dismissal.

---

40 Exo 20:2-14; 21:5; Lev 19:18,34; Deu 5:6-18; 10-12;13:4; 30:6,16.
41 Mat 22:37-39; Mark 12:30-31; Luke 10:27.

On the other hand, we know that we cannot fully keep all of the commandments, and that breaking the Law called for a sacrifice. Moreover, if we were living under the Law, we would have been stoned to death for breaking many of its commands. [42] Thus, apart from our Messiah and His sacrifice on our behalf, we are but "dead men walking." We have been weighed and found wanting and now await our execution date. Without Salvation (Yeshua), we are dead in our trespasses, because the wages of sin are death. We therefore approach the precepts of Torah as men who have been tried, found guilty, and put to death for our sins. Yet, at the same time, we have been redeemed from the curse of death that comes from breaking the Law. In Messiah we rejoice because in Him, in spirit, we have already begun to be raised from the dead: We were "made to die to the law through the body of Messiah, that we might be joined to another, to Him who was raised from the dead, in order that we might bear fruit for God" (Rom 6:23; 7:4).

If we look to the Law for our salvation, we are deceived. If we seek to establish our righteousness by keeping the Law, we must keep the whole Law and return to the Mosaic system of sacrifice. But we cannot do that. Abba allowed the Temple to be destroyed after His Son paid the price for our sins (1 Pet 1:18-19). We cannot offer the required animal sacrifices. Yet, we must emulate Messiah, who said: "Do not think that I came to abolish the law or the prophets; I did not come to abolish but to fulfill" (Mat 5:17). Yeshua came to fulfill (satisfy) the sacrificial requirements of the Law once and for all. [43] He came to fully preach and perfect it, to personify how it is to be walked out by man. And, if we say we abide in Him, we "ought to walk in the same manner as He walked" (1 John 2:6).

---

[42] Exo 21:12,16,17; 21:29; 22:19; 31:14, 15; Lev 20:2,11,13,27; 24:16; Num 3:10; 15:35; Deu 13:10; 17:5; 21:21; 22:21; 22:24. See *Mama's Torah*, Wootten, page 87.

[43] Fulfill: *Strong's* # G 4134. Rom 6:10; Heb 7:27; 9:12; 10:10;1 Pet 3:18; Jude 1:3. See *Redeemed Israel*, Wootten, chapter 28, "The Law and New Covenant Believers."

MAKING A COMMITMENT

TWELVE

MAKING A COMMITMENT

Yeshua said many things about the commandments. Such as: If you love Me, keep My commandments — If anyone loves Me, he will keep My word— The word which you hear is not Mine, but the Father's who sent Me — And, If you keep My commandments, you will abide in My love; just as I have kept My Father's commandments, and abide in His love. [44]

These things were said by One who also said, "Do not think I came to abolish the law or the prophets; I did not come to abolish, but to fulfill." For, "not the smallest stroke of the law will pass away until all is fulfilled" (Mat 5:17,18).

"All" is not fulfilled: Scattered Israel is not fully regathered, circumcised of heart, keeping all the Law; and Messiah's foot has not yet touched down on the Mount of Olives. [45]

Thus, the Father's Law must still be in force.

---

[44] John 14:15,23,24; 15:10.
[45] Zech 14:4; Deu 30:1-9; 33, Ezek 37:15-28; 44:9.

Many Believers teach that we are not "under the Law," and they are right in that we are no longer under the *sacrificial Laws*. For, "when the priesthood is changed, of necessity the law is changed also." The priesthood was changed from that of the Aaronic order to that of the order of Melchizedek when Messiah our Passover was sacrificed. [46] He redeemed us from the "curse" of death that comes from breaking the Law (Gal 3:13). His Blood delivers us from the "penalty" due lawbreakers. However, the Father's Laws, or, *Loving Instructions*, comprise eternal principles— from which we will never be delivered. And neither should we want to be delivered from them.

We cannot enter into the *Laolum Haba*, the Eternal Kingdom to Come, without first embracing the laws that: We will have no other gods. We will honor our father and our mother. We will not lie, cheat, steal, bear false witness, practice sorcery, murder, commit adultery, cohabit with animals or those of the same sex, etc. Furthermore, desire to do these things must not even be entertained in our hearts! [47] Our Messiah said, "Whoever then annuls one of the least of these commandments, and so teaches others, shall be called least in the kingdom of heaven; but whoever keeps and teaches them, he shall be called great in the kingdom of heaven" (Mat 5:19).

Christianity short-changes itself by not teaching that Torah is full of ancient truths that help make men wise. Believers are robbed when they do not embrace truths that make for a rewarding way of life. They are misled, not realizing that "the law is spiritual" (Rom 7:14). [48] And they miss the fact that, "Where there is no law, there is no transgression" (Rom 4:15). For sinners to repent, of necessity, there must be a law they need to repent of having broken.

---

[46] Heb 7:1-28; 1 Cor 5:7.
[47] 1 Cor 5:7; Gal 3:13. Matt 5:22,28; Rev 22:15.
[48] See, *Take Two Tablets Daily: A Survey of the Ten Commandments and 613 Laws*, by Angus Wootten, Key of David Publishing.

Making A Commitment

The Law must be upheld, for without it, man cannot know grace, which is forgiveness and unmerited favor.

Those who know Yeshua would not change a thing about Him. His earthly walk was the perfect role model for all— Jew and non-Jew alike. We follow Yeshua, Who kept the Law, yet was and is grace personified. We therefore walk as He walked, not seeking to destroy, but to fulfill.

Doctrines That Do Not Hold Water

Our Father prayed that we might have a "heart" for His commandments. They are the water with which we are to wash ourselves. Let us, therefore, not ever forsake them (Deu 5:29; 11:8; Eph 5:26; Jer 2:13; 17:13).

Claiming "they are not under the law," many create Church by-laws, dogmas, doctrines and decrees— which often hold no water when measured against the Word. They forget that He warned: "Do not walk in the statutes of your fathers, or keep their ordinances, or defile yourselves with their idols. I am the Lord your GOD; walk in My statutes, and keep My ordinances, and observe them" (Eze 20:18-20). Yet, Abba had to say of our forefathers, "They have polluted My land…with their abominations." Thus, we must admit that we have inherited their lies, vanity, and things wherein there is no profit (Jer 16:17-19).

Like our fathers and their falsehoods, we will not be able to say to the Holy One, "I followed the doctrines and decrees of my Church, so please judge me according to those rules." No. We will be judged according to His Word.

Our God will soon purge from among us all transgressors. Those who remain will truly know Him. To live on His Holy Mountain we will have to serve according to His Word. His standards are high, and the LORD of Hosts is now bringing forth an obedient army. We want to be members of that mighty army (Jer 31:31-33; Eze 20:32-44).

The Voice... Hearing the Almighty

Principles For Growing In Messiah

Yeshua "came to seek and to save that which was lost" (Luke 19:10). He came to restore our lost fellowship with the Holy One. [49] He did this because the Father wants to talk with us on a personal level. When He has to, He will use human mediators: prophets, pastors, and even donkeys. But in the end, there is "but one mediator between God and man, the man Messiah Yeshua" (1 Tim 2:5).

YHVH does not want us to need someone else to tell us what He wants. Nor does He want us to fear hearing His voice. He instead wants us to grow up in Messiah. [50]

Personal maturation is what our sojourn in this earthly wilderness is about. We need to grow up because in the days ahead we will need to have ears to hear when He says, "This is the way, walk ye in it" (Isa 30:21, KJV).

It is good to have the benefits of fellowship and proper regard for the Church, but we also know that the last-days Laodicean church ultimately degenerates into a godless shell, having a form of godliness but denying the power thereof. Then, she will be spit out of the Messiah's mouth.

We do not want to be in her when that happens.

As for study, we do it to show ourselves approved unto God, a workman that does not need to be ashamed, but rightly divides the word of truth. However, we also must be diligent about seeking the Spirit (1 Cor 2:10; 2 Tim 2:15). We cannot obtain the giftings of the Spirit through intellectual pursuits alone. It is the Spirit of God who teaches us "the depths of God." The Spirit imparts wisdom that is greater than man's wisdom. By intellect alone, man cannot discover these things. Yeshua's wisdom includes mysteries that are hidden from the world, but revealed through His Spirit (1 Cor 1:25; 2:6-9).

---

49 Isa 49:6,8; Jer 29:14; 30:3; 33:7; Ezek 39:25; Amos 9:14; Zech 9:12; Acts 15:16.
50 Exo 20:19; Deu 18:16; 1Sam 8:5-7; Eph 4:15.

MAKING A COMMITMENT

The Psalmist said Messiah would open His mouth in parables and utter hidden things from of old (Psa 78:1-7).

Yeshua often spoke in parables. To those who could not hear, His were but simple stories. For those who did hear, His parables imparted principles by which one could live life. His stories were filled with treasures, gems that brought to life the glories of the Kingdom (Mat 13:10-17).

Our objective in assembling together should not be to garner more human learning, but to come to intimately know our God— by His Spirit. And, as scary as the thought might be, in our corporate gatherings we should desire to hear the voice of the LORD. For we want Him to guide us individually *and corporately*. Yeshua said His sheep *would* hear His voice. He promised that the Spirit *would* speak to us. Peter and John listened to the voice of God *more so than the voices of men*— and they boldly spoke of the things they heard (John 10:27; 16:12-14, 25; Acts 4:19-20).

We want to hear and obey Him, too.

Solid food is said to be for the mature, for those who have their spiritual senses trained to discern both good and evil. Yeshua said, "My *food* is to do the will of Him who sent Me and to accomplish His work" (Heb 5:14; John 4:34). The milk of the Gospel is for babes. Solid food, which is *doing* the work of the Father, is for the mature— for those who know how to hear the Holy Spirit.

We want to be well-trained workers.

We also want to be pure in heart. Desire for a pure heart is not equal to having one. Good intentions are not enough. We must love YHVH with all our heart, soul, and might. He must have the preeminent place in our heart and life. We must not allow anything to come before Him. We therefore need to purpose in our hearts to release to Him everything that is precious to us. For, in giving Him our all, we gain entrance into His abundant kingdom.

We now want to forsake all and follow Him.

The Woman in the Wilderness

"A great sign appeared in heaven: a woman clothed with the sun, and the moon under her feet, and on her head a crown of twelve stars. ...And the woman fled into the wilderness where she had a place prepared by God, so that there she might be nourished for one thousand two hundred and sixty days ...And the two wings of the great eagle were given to the woman, in order that she might fly into the wilderness to her place, where she was nourished for a time and times and half a time, from the presence of the serpent" (Rev 12:1,6,14).

In this picture we see the woman, Israel, with twelve stars that symbolize her Twelve Tribes. In her we see the true *church/ekklesia*: She was in the wilderness in the Old Covenant (Acts 7:38) and is presently in the wilderness of the Nations. Clothed with the sun/Son, she overcomes darkness.

We want to be part of her as she overcomes darkness.

We do not want to be part of the harlot who is betrothed to the beast: "He carried me away in the Spirit into a wilderness; and I saw a woman sitting on a scarlet beast, full of blasphemous names" (Rev 17:3). Because of her blasphemy, "the Lord has a controversy with the nations." He enters into judgment with all flesh. He gives the wicked to the sword. "I will gather all the nations," He says, "And bring them down to the valley of Jehoshaphat. Then I will enter into judgment with them there" (Jer 25:31; Joel 3:2).

Of that day YHVH says, "Multitudes, multitudes in the valley of decision! For the day of the Lord is near in the valley of decision" (Joel 3:14).

There are only two roads that lead out of this valley: One goes to Babylon, to the Harlot, and to union with the Beast. The other road leads to Jerusalem.

We want to take the Road to Jerusalem.

Making A Commitment

Finding Grace In The Wilderness

YHVH says, "The people who survived the sword found grace in the wilderness— Israel, when it went to find its rest" (Jer 31:2). According to *Soncino Books of the Bible*, "the people left of the sword [are], ...the survivors of the Northern Kingdom." [51]

Ephraim, the *melo hagoyim*, at last, their wilderness affliction begins to produce grace in them. YHVH says, then, "As a soothing aroma I shall accept you, when I bring you out from the peoples and gather you from the lands where you are scattered" (Gen 48:19; Rom 11:25; Eze 20:41).

In the wilderness, Yah "brings us under the bond of the covenant" (Eze 20:37). This speaks of our reconsecration as YHVH's people. When He pours out His Spirit on us, our wilderness becomes a fertile field, even a forest. As we submit to His purging, we find justice and righteousness; the wilderness and desert are made glad and rejoice and blossom (Isa 32:15-16; 35:1). YHVH then opens rivers and springs and makes the wilderness a pool of water, and dry land becomes fountains. There, His Glory will appear. He gives drink to His chosen people. He will speak and make His oracles come alive. He will comfort Zion and all her waste places. Her wilderness He will make like Eden, her desert like the garden of the LORD; joy and gladness will be found in her (Isa 41:18; 43:20; 51:3; Exo 16:10; Acts 7:38).

We want to be counted among that people.

Behold! I Do A New Thing

Our Father is doing a new thing in the earth.

> "'Hear the word of the Lord, O house of Jacob, and all the families of the house of Israel... At that

---

[51] *Soncino Books of the Bible*, NY, 1978, Ezekiel 20:37 comment, p 129.

time,' declares YHVH, 'I will be the God of all the families of Israel, and they shall be My people... Behold, I will do something new, now it will spring forth; will you not be aware of it? I will even make a roadway in the wilderness" (Jer 2:4; 31:1; Isa 43:19).

We want to walk on that roadway.

Responding to the Call

The word of YHVH for us in this hour is, "Not by might nor by power, but by My Spirit" (Zec 4:6).

It is now time for us to respond to the Father's call to help rebuild His nation— it is time for us to work to reunite David's divided house— it is time to declare that Torah will be the history and constitution of our restored house— and it is time to be clothed with power from on High, by the Ruach haKodesh.

We are living in the time of the restoration of all things.

True restoration will come, not by the might of man, but through the true power that is found in the Holy Spirit.

Thus, it is time for us to make a commitment.

Yeshua said, the Holy Spirit "will teach you all things, and bring to your remembrance all that I said to you." If we are being tried, we are not to fear, but remember Yeshua's promise: "The Holy Spirit will teach you in that very hour what you ought to say." We abide in the Spirit, and His anointing teaches us (John 14:26; Luke 12:12; 1 John 2:27).

The Ruach haKodesh is the One appointed to lead, teach, and guide us, as we journey toward our end goal— the *Olam Haba*, the Eternal Kingdom.

Father God, We stand before You and give You our all— everything. We withhold nothing. We ask that You please take our hearts now. And we ask that, in Your mercy, You might lead us safely through the wilderness and home to You.

Amen and Amen.

Thirteen

The Best Is Yet to Come!

The following message was delivered by retired school teacher, Merle Rawlings, at a Messianic Israel Alliance Conference in Salt Lake City in 2006.

In it, Mr. Rawlings offers a glimpse of what is yet to come for those who seek Israel's full restoration. It is here reproduced based on the notes from his talk.

Just before His Ascension, Yeshua told his apostles "not to depart from Jerusalem, but to wait for the Promise of the Father." The Promise was that they would "receive power" and be witnesses to Yeshua beginning at Jerusalem and finally extending "to the end of the earth" (Acts 1:4,8).

In Acts 2 the Promise was wonderfully fulfilled:

"A sound from heaven, as of a rushing mighty wind" filled "the whole house" and "tongues, as of fire…sat upon each of them." The disciples were all filled with the Holy Spirit and began to speak with other tongues— the languages of devout men from every nation under heaven (Acts 2:2-5).

Peter referred to Joel's prophecy in Acts 2:17-21 to explain to the crowd that had gathered what was happening:

> "And it shall come to pass in the last days, says God, that I will pour out of My Spirit on all flesh; your sons and your daughters shall prophecy, your young men shall see visions, your old men shall dream dreams. And on My menservants and on My maidservants I will pour out My Spirit in those days; and they shall prophecy. I will show wonders in heaven above and signs in the earth beneath: blood and fire and vapor of smoke. The sun shall be turned into darkness, and the moon into blood, before the coming of the great and awesome day of the Lord. And it shall come to pass that whoever calls on the name of the Lord shall be saved."

As we consider the momentous event recorded in Acts 2, we need to ask ourselves, *"Did these signs and wonders mentioned in verses 19-20 come to pass in Peter's day?"*

No, they did not. There was no "blood and fire," no "vapor of smoke." Nor was the "sun turned into darkness," nor "the moon into blood." This part of Joel's prophecy is reserved for the "last days." Perhaps Joel was writing of *our* day, the day of Israel's regathering.

What happened in Acts 2:2-4 was certainly a partial fulfillment of Joel's prophecy, as quoted by Peter at the Feast of Shavuot in Jerusalem. However, the rest of Joel's prophecy is yet to be fulfilled. It is a "double-fulfillment prophecy," and for us, that means the best is yet to come!

The intrepid Joel foretells yet another outpouring of the Holy Spirit, and that outpouring coincides with, and even energizes, Israel's future regathering.

Acts 2:17: "And it shall come to pass in the last days says God, that I will pour out of My Spirit on all flesh..."

This is slated to happen in our day— "in the last days."

This great outpouring will mark the second and final fulfillment of Joel's prophecy. With this outpouring, every detail spoken of by Joel in these verses quoted by Peter shall completely come to pass.

As if to emphasize the "last days" fulfillment of Joel's prophecy, Peter quotes definite, relevant signs of the "last days." These most unusual, yet specific signs include "blood and fire" and "vapor of smoke." In addition, "the sun shall be turned into darkness, and the moon into blood, before the coming of the great and awesome day of the Lord" (Acts 2:19-20).

The early church experienced a partial fulfillment of the prophesied "pouring out" of the Holy Spirit, and it is recorded in Acts 2. However, we are about to witness the final or complete fulfillment of Joel's prophecy, a veritable "rest of the story." For Messiah's followers around the world, the best is yet to come!

A Future Outpouring

Consider this example of prophetic events that we have to expect. Ezekiel, writing some 2,500 years ago, informs us of a unique, future outpouring of the Holy Spirit. Chapter 37 begins with the prophet being placed in the midst of a valley full of bones— very many bones that were very dry. The bones that Ezekiel saw had been lifeless for a very long time— for over 2,000 years!

During the conversation the Lord had with Ezekiel about these dry bones, the Lord said, "'I will put My Spirit in you, and you shall live, and I will place you in your own land. Then you shall know that I, the Lord, have spoken it and performed it,' says the Lord" (Eze 37:14).

All the rest of the promises foretold in that chapter are contingent on the Holy Spirit giving life to the very many, very dry bones— which bones represent the "whole house of Israel."

Again, this event is to happen in our day—in the "last days." Specifically, the promise is that the Holy Spirit will breathe life into bone-dry dispersed Israel, and He will facilitate the regathering that places them once again in their own land. The powerful Presence of the Holy Spirit is the catalyst for all the tremendous blessings that follow.

Yet another example of the Holy Spirit's involvement in a "last days" event is the spiritual cleansing and redemption of Israel prophesied in Ezekiel 36:24-27:

> "For I will take you from among the nations, gather you out of all countries, and bring you into your own land. Then I will sprinkle clean water on you, and you shall be clean; I will cleanse you from all your filthiness and from all your idols. I will give you a new heart and put a new spirit within you; I will take the heart of stone out of your flesh and give you a heart of flesh. I will put My Spirit within you and cause you to walk in My statutes, and you will keep My judgments and do them."

The Holy Spirit is still in the business of cleansing hearts, but this time, an entire nation gathered from the four corners of the earth is cleansed. They are a rather scruffy, dry-bones bunch to begin with, but look at the results of the Holy Spirit's transformation of regathered Israel in the next verse: "Then you shall dwell in the land that I gave to your fathers; you shall be My people, and I will be your God."

We find a third example of Joel's prophecy seeing a second fulfillment in the "last days." Ezekiel 39:29 tells us, "And I will not hide My face from them anymore; for I shall have poured out my Spirit on the house of Israel, says the Lord." Joel's prophecy, as quoted by Peter in Acts 2:17, reads, "And it shall come to pass in the last days says God, that I will pour out of My Spirit..."

Ezekiel and Joel use the same phrase. The Lord says, when He regathers cleansed Israel: "I shall have poured out My Spirit..."

NEW COVENANT IMPLICATIONS

There is another double-fulfillment prophecy in the Bible that relates directly to the "last days" examples from Ezekiel. This one is Jeremiah's famous "New Covenant" prophecy. It tells us about the practical, long term outcome of the Holy Spirit being poured out on regathered Israel:

> "But this is the covenant that I will make with the house of Israel after those days, says the Lord: I will put My law in their minds, and write it on their hearts; and I will be their God, and they shall be My people. No more shall every man teach his neighbor, and every man his brother, saying, know the Lord, for they all shall know Me, from the least of them to the greatest of them, says the Lord. For I will forgive their iniquity, and their sin I will remember no more" (Jer 31:33-34; also see Heb 8:8-13).

Finally, redeemed and restored Israel will enjoy the fullness of the New Covenant, as a direct result of the cleansing and empowering Presence of the Holy Spirit among them. For the first time in recorded history, every citizen of a nation (Israel) will live out the eternal principles of Torah with understanding, integrity, and joy. Israelites regathered from around the world will love the Father and choose to carefully and completely live for Him.

The complete fulfillment of Joel's "last days" prophecy quoted by Peter will literally rewrite Israel's history:

> "Behold, the days are coming, says the Lord, that it shall no more be said, the Lord lives who brought up the children of Israel from Egypt, but, the Lord

lives who brought up the children from the land of the north and from all the lands where He had driven them. For I will bring them back into their land which I gave to their fathers" (Jer 16:14-15).

The results of the outpouring of the Holy Spirit in these "last days" are as follows:

- Israel is regathered from every nation to their own land
- Israel is cleansed and redeemed by the Holy Spirit.
- Israel then reckons its founding from her regathering, cleansing, and the Spirit's Presence over the entire nation
- Israel then enjoys the New Covenant implemented in its entirety

What does all this mean for us today? Israelites asked something like this previously: *"...Men and brethren, what shall we do?"* (Acts 2:37)

First, we who are already involved in the Messianic movement have a great responsibility as pioneers and forerunners. Early in the last century, many Jewish settlers returning to Israel did not live to see the political rebirth of the nation in 1948, but their hard work, vision, and determination laid the foundation for a modern, viable Israel. It's much like that with us today and with this understanding in mind, we must press forward, realizing that the regathering of Israel in our day is not just another "movement." It is THE movement or work of the Holy Spirit before Messiah Yeshua returns.

Second, we need to know, love, and share our faith. Peter admonished the "pilgrims of the Dispersion," to "always be ready to give a defense to everyone who asks you a reason for the hope that is in you" (1 Pet 1:1; 3:15). Peter and the apostles shared the Good News on a person-to-person basis with anyone who would listen. It's still a wonderfully effective method of sharing, and it causes the devil much heartburn and loss of sleep.

Third, we are the Messianic "newspaper." When people "read" us, what information or model do they perceive? Hopefully, we reflect the living, walking Torah: Messiah Yeshua. He said, "By this shall all men know you are My disciples, if you have love for one another" (John 13:35).

There is a sound reason why Sister Batya, in virtually every MIA conference, pleads for us to "be merciful with each other." Love and mercy are compatible and both are essential for Israel's regathering.

Fourth, unity is an observable, natural outcome of love. Unity has been likened to the Holy Spirit's anointing in Psalm 133. The "precious oil" and the "dew of Hermon" are metaphors of the Holy Spirit. Where the Holy Spirit is, there's not only liberty, there are brethren dwelling together in unity. And, lest we forget, unity is a fundamental characteristic of our Messiah's future Bride.

May we, too, receive generously of the "precious oil" and the "dew of Hermon" as we move forward in Israel's regathering. "The times of restoration of all things" (Acts 3:21) are before us— and that clearly includes having the Holy Spirit "poured out" on regathered, cleansed Israel in the "last days."

Surely the best is yet to come!

The Voice... Hearing the Almighty

FOURTEEN

Voices in Scripture

Psalm 29 is a beloved Psalm. In preparation for the Sabbath it is a Jewish custom to meditate on this text. It was chosen by the rabbis because of its emphasis on the majesty of our God, and on His voice. In these verses, seven times David repeated the expression *"hakol Adonai"* (The voice of the Lord/YHVH). The powerful words of this Psalm encourage worship, and devotion to the Almighty.

King David declared of the King of Kings:

> "The voice of YHVH is powerful,
> "The voice of YHVH is majestic
> "The voice of YHVH breaks the cedars;
> "Yes, YHVH breaks in pieces the cedars of Lebanon.
> "The voice of YHVH hews out flames of fire.
> "The voice of YHVH shakes the wilderness;
> "YHVH shakes the wilderness of Kadesh.
> "The voice of YHVH makes the deer to calve and strips the forests bare; and in His temple everything says, 'Glory!'" (Psa 29:4-9).

The Voice... Hearing the Almighty

Verses About Voices

- "Has YHVH as much delight in burnt offerings and sacrifices as in obeying the voice of YHVH? Behold, to obey is better than sacrifice, and to heed than the fat of rams" (1 Sam 15:22).
  We who wish to honor the feasts of the Lord, His Torah, and His Messiah, must realize that YHVH puts great emphasis on our "heeding" His voice.
- "Behold," says Messiah Yeshua, "I stand at the door and knock; if anyone hears My voice and opens the door, I will come in to him and will dine with him, and he with Me" (Rev 3:20).
  Messiah Yeshua likewise wants us to listen to His voice— which will always sound in unison with His Father because they are "One" (John 10:30).
- "Today if you hear His voice, harden not your hearts" (Psa 95:8; Heb 3:7,8).
  When we hear Abba's voice, like a little child, out of great respect for our father we immediately say, "Yes, Daddy." We must not procrastinate and thereby let the moment of His blessing pass us by.
- "YHVH utters His voice before His army; surely His camp is very great, for strong is he who carries out His word. The day of YHVH is indeed great and very awesome" (Joel 2:11).
  To be part of His great army, to be made strong, we must believe that every utterance of *YHVH Tsava'ot* (the Lord of Hosts) is sure and will be carried out.
- "Get yourself up on a high mountain, O Zion, bearer of good news, lift up your voice mightily, O Jerusalem..., lift it up, do not fear. Say to the cities of Judah, 'Here is your God!'" (Isa 40:9).
  We are not to fear, but to proclaim salvation—which is found in *Yeshua*. His very Name means *Salvation*.

- "In the beginning God created the heavens and the earth. The earth was formless and void.... Then God *said*, 'Let there be light,' and there was light" (Gen 1:1-3).

  Inherent *power* is in the speech of the Almighty: He *spoke*, and it was so. Our God is holy, as is His speech. To hear His voice is a gift to be treasured above all else. His voice is not to be feared, but revered. We do not run from it, but toward it.

- "Who shall ascend into the hill of YHVH or who shall stand in His holy place? He that has clean hands, and a pure heart; who has not lifted up his soul unto vanity, nor sworn deceitfully. He shall receive the blessing from YHVH, and righteousness from the Elohim of his salvation. This is the generation of them that seek Him, that seek thy face, O Jacob. Selah" (Psa 24:3-6, KJV).

  We must have clean hands and a pure heart and not swear deceitfully. We must stand for the truth.

- "Listen to Me, you who follow after righteousness, you who seek YHVH: Look to the rock from which you were hewn, and to the hole of the pit from which you were dug. Look to Abraham your father, and to Sarah who bore you; for I called him alone, and blessed him and increased him" (Isa 51:1-2).

  If we want to hear the Fathers voice, we must look to the positive examples of our forefathers. We must have a simple, yet determined faith like that of Abraham, Isaac, and Jacob/Israel.

- YHVH speaks of a *voice* that is heard in Ramah; it is one of lamentation, and bitter weeping. It is Rachel weeping for her children— who were Joseph and Benjamin. Joseph's son, Ephraim became the leader of the Northern Kingdom of Israel, and Benjamin was with Judah. Mother Rachel weeps for both houses, and YHVH says to her: "Restrain your voice from weeping and your eyes from tears; for... they will return...There is hope for your future.... Your children will return to their own territory." When Rachel's children begin their return, YHVH hears "Ephraim grieving." He admits to having been like "an untrained calf," and when he is "instructed" about his own Israelite roots, he bears the reproach of his youth. Then, YHVH calls him His "dear son," His "delightful child" (Jer 31:15-21). YHVH rewarded Rachel's weeping. We need to raise our voice in weeping even as she did. We need to cry out, "Set up for yourself roadmarks, place for yourself guideposts; direct your mind to the highway, the way by which you went. Return, O virgin of Israel, Return to these your cities." We need to pray that Ephraim might learn to walk in his call as "Firstborn Israel" (Jer 31:8-9,21).

BABEL AND TOWERS TO SELF

In Scripture study, there is a generally accepted "Law of First Use," meaning, the first time a word is used, it sets a standard. And the first time we see a form of *speech* in Scripture is, "In the beginning God created the heavens and the earth. The earth was formless and void.... Then God *said*, 'Let there be light,' and there was light" (Gen 1:1-3). [52] Again we note the inherent and *holy power* of the speech of our God: He *spoke*, and it was so. He *created good* when He *spoke*. We also note that in the Garden He breathed the breath of life into man, and He equipped him with the incomparable gift of intelligible words and speech. Abba created us above the animals and granted that we, too, might know some of language's creative power.

---

[52] Said: S&BDB word # H 559, *amar*: to say, speak, talk.

Then we fell. We found that we were *naked*. Like the serpent who deceived us with cunning words, we, too, became *cunning*. So Abba "drove the man out; and at the east of the garden of Eden He stationed the cherubim and the flaming sword which turned every direction to guard the way to the tree of life" (Gen 3:1,24). Abba forced us to leave His Garden, lest in our cunning state, we should eat of the Tree of Life and live forever.

Man then began to populate the earth, and all men used the same language and words. They could accomplish much because they understood each other's speech. Then a certain sin again reared its ugly head. Man wanted to make a "name" for himself, so he built himself a city.

In the story of the Tower of Babel, we see that the word translated *city* means a place guarded by *waking* or *a watch*. It is rooted in the word, *uwr* [oor], and carries with it the idea of *opening the eyes*, of *lifting up self*, and, *to be made naked* (Gen 11:1-9). [53]

Again, we remember that Adam saw that he was *naked*, and that the word used is related to the idea of being *cunning*. [54] In Adam and in his offspring, we see the same sin, spreading and growing. In various ways, it is all tied to the idea of *cunning speech*, speech that lifts up man and not the Almighty God.

In this same dismally-fated city (ultimately named "Babel"), man created a "tower." To stop our unified trek toward destruction, Abba confounded our languages. At Babel, man began to "babble."

The babble of man's confused state has confounded him ever since. He no longer spoke the acceptable language of the Garden...

---

53 *S&BDB* word #'s H 5892 and 5782-83.
54 *S&BDB* word # H 6191. aram, aw-ram'; a prim. root; prop. to be (or make) bare; but used only in the der. sense (through the idea perh. of smoothness) to be cunning (usually in a bad sense):-- X very, beware, take crafty [counsel], be prudent, deal subtilly. Gen 3:7.

The Voice... Hearing the Almighty

In His mercy, Abba confounded our languages to keep us from building "towers" to our own name. The Hebrew word translated *tower*, is *migdal* and can be used to describe a *pulpit*. Rooted in the word *gadal*, when used in its negative sense, it can mean to lift up (as in pride), to boast, or to speak proudly. [55]

When man uses a "bully pulpit" to lift himself up, he is participating in an ancient sin. People who use the power of pulpits to pummel others will, one day, be punished. Permanently.

Position should never be used to lift up self. We do not hear such words from the One who spoke the World into existence. Like our Creator, our speech should be used to create, to affect good in the earth. To use our voice in an unholy way, to disparage our God, or others, defiles His precious gift. Thus, Proverbs 25:11 tells us, "A word fitly spoken is like apples of gold in pictures of silver."

Aptly spoken words can make a positive difference in the life of others. We therefore want to be careful with, and to diligently guard, our speech.

Speech is powerful, and we want our speech, our words, to be fit for the Garden of Eden. Speech also is inextricably linked to having authority. [56] Our Messiah conferred His authority on us, and to properly represent Him, we need to regard speech even as He regarded it. [57]

Voices and Choices

It is imperative that we realize our need to hear our Heavenly Father's voice. We need to invite the Ruach into our lives, *now*. We have entered into a season that will prove to be both dangerous and glorious.

---

[55] *S&BDB* word #'s H 4026 and 1431.
[56] Mat 28:18-20; Mark 1:27; 2:10-11; Luke 4:36; 7:7.
[57] Mat 5:37; 21:43-45; Luke 22:28-30; Heb 12:28.

VOICES IN SCRIPTURE

Difficult days are at our door, and each of us needs to learn to clearly hear the voice of the Holy One. For He promises His faithful ones, *"Your ears will hear a word behind you, 'This is the way, walk in it.'"*

Our God will speak to us, and regardless of our situation, we will know whether to turn right or left. Because He has spoken to us, we will know the way in which we should go (Isa 30:21).

When the enemy of our soul, the serpent of old who is called the devil and Satan, is "thrown down to the earth, " he comes with "great wrath, knowing that he has only a short time."

At that time, he especially seeks to destroy reunited Israel. He comes after Believers with a vengeance. Our ability to stay safe and nourished will have much to do with our ability to hear and obey the Holy One during such trying times (Rev 12:9-14).

The voice of the enemy ever seeks to lure us away from our God. The Ruach ever seeks to draw us near to Him. The Ruach encourages us to listen to the Father's voice alone, which will keep us safe.

We are given the gift of free will, and so must choose which voice we will listen to.

House of Israel, let us choose this day whom we will serve.
Let us beseech our God to give us ears to hear His voice.

The Voice... Hearing the Almighty

Fifteen

Kol Ba'Midbar

Kol Ba'Midbar is Hebrew for "Voice in the Wilderness." In Isaiah 40:3 we read of a voice that calls out:

> "Clear the way for the LORD in the wilderness; make smooth in the desert, a highway for our God. Let every valley be lifted up, and every mountain and hill be made low; let the rough ground become a plain, and the rugged terrain a broad valley; Then the glory of the LORD will be revealed, and all flesh will see it together; for the mouth of the LORD has spoken" (Isa 40:3-5).

Matthew said of John the Baptist (or Immerser), "This is the one referred to by Isaiah the prophet when he said, the voice of one crying in the wilderness, 'Make ready the way of the LORD, make his paths straight!'" (Mat 3:3).

The Father spoke of a time when He would bring the children of Israel into "the wilderness of the peoples." And, He said, at that time, "I shall enter into judgment with them face to face." Furthermore, "I shall make you pass under the rod, and I shall bring you into the bond of the covenant; and I shall purge from you the rebels and those who transgress against Me" (Eze 20:35-38).

Those who presently feel lost, alone, or alienated from organized religion would do well to glean from these verses about this desert experience. In them is found food for hungry souls, drink for parched spirits, and a way of escape for Israelites who want to flee all godless wastelands (Eze 20:11-44).

What is the "wilderness of the peoples"?

"Wilderness" is translated from the Hebrew word *midbar*, it being the word for *desert*— which often is described negatively: without grapes/wine, pools of water, or pleasant places. [58] For this reason, the Psalmist asks a question that seems to have a self-evident answer, "Can God furnish a table in the wilderness?" (Psa 78:19). In other words, it is such a barren place, that one wonders if even God Himself can supply in it.

"People" is translated from the Hebrew, *am*. YHVH uses this word when He calls His people "*Ammi*," which means, "My people" (Hos 2:23,25).

According to the *Theological Wordbook of the Old Testament*, *am* expresses "the unity of the group." [59] Unified religious organizations, such as churches, synagogues, home fellowships, and ministries, are "groups of people." Moreover, beyond doubt, some of these groups have little of the "water of the Word"— and many Believers find themselves lost in such parched wastelands. [60]

The "wilderness of the peoples" speaks of dry, desert experiences. It speaks of our being in a group that is without water or wine, and it is not a pleasant place.

---

[58] *TWOT*, word # 399, page 181.
[59] *TWOT* word # 1640, page 676; *S&BDB* # H5971.
[60] Eph 5:26; Rev 3:17; 2 Tim 3:5,12.

We would do well to realize that Abba brings us into this place for a reason: "There," He says, "I will confront *you*. There will I state My case against *you*" (New English Bible). "I will deal with *you* there face to face" (Moffatt).

It is as was stated in an old *Pogo* cartoon: "I have seen the enemy, and it is *us!*"

We are the ones whom the Lord seeks to isolate at this time. It is still a matter of "If *My* people..."

Of this wilderness encounter, *Soncino Books of the Bible* says, "As in the wilderness of Egypt they were constituted the people of God, so in this desert, cut off from intercourse with heathen nations, they will be made again into His people. There, God will *plead*, i.e. remonstrate and reason with them, face to face with none to distract their attention from Him."[61]

YHVH has a history of bringing His people to a place of isolation and dealing with them there. So it is that He is dealing with many in the same way in this last day.

Ezekiel does not speak of congregational confrontation, but of a personal encounter. In the wilderness, the Holy One cuts off the bonds between heathen and Israelite. He isolates us. When we flounder among a sea of peoples, the Father begins to deal with us— individually.

In the desert, He also teaches us to sing a certain song, it being, *"Though none go with me, still I will follow..."*

When we can sing this song about our relationship with Him, when, in our heart there is "no turning back," we become a force the world has to reckon with. In this way, we learn to stand, even if it means we must stand alone.

However, our Father's plan is not that we might forever stand alone, but that we might become committed to being citizens of His kingdom, His chosen nation. YHVH wants this because, to this day, He longs for a set-apart nation that belongs solely to Him.

---

[61] *Soncino Books of the Bible*, NY, 1978, Ezekiel 20:35 comment, p 129.

A Time Of Testing And Grieving

As for our being gathered as His people, the Father long-ago swore, "I will gather those who grieve about the appointed feasts— They came from you, O Zion, and the reproach of exile is a burden on them" (Zep 3:18).

While lost in a dry desert of idolatry, the children of Zion will grieve for the pure unadulterated feasts of Israel. They will regard the idea of being separated from the Land promised to the Fathers as a "reproach." They will long for the true comfort of Shabbat. In seeking true reunion with their God, they will turn from all Gentilized, heathen, and false religious practices— be they Jewish or non-Jewish traditions. If the practices are unscriptural, these repentant ones will turn from them (Deu 13:1-5). And, in turning away, they will be made to feel alienated and alone.

For those who seek to return to the truth of Scripture, it will be as difficult as Messiah warned that it would be. Households will be divided, father against son and son against father, mother against daughter and daughter against mother, mother-in-law against daughter-in-law and daughter-in- law against mother-in-law (Luke 12:51-53).

Why does Abba bring His children into this hard place?

So "that He might humble you, testing you, to know what is in your heart." *Testing is the reason for the season.*

At times, Abba allows us to be *tested by false prophets and wonder workers*— to see if we will go after them, or purge them and their iniquity from our midst (Deu 8:2; 13:1-5).

Desert time is test time. While there, Believers need to grow up in Messiah and move beyond the elementary fundamentals of our faith: Repentance, faith, baptisms, laying on of hands, resurrection, and eternal judgment— and to advance (Eph 4:15; Heb 6:1-3). If we are not diligent about moving beyond the *necessary— yet elementary truths of our faith*— we become, slothful, sluggish, bored.

YHVH wants to instead excite us. He wants to make unmistakably clear to Abraham's heirs His unswerving determination to fulfill His promise. He wants us to see that *we* have always been part of His plan, and that *we* are very much a part of His plan in this hour. But... most churches have not moved beyond these elementary principles— which causes many to feel like they are being pastured in a desert wasteland (Heb 6:12,17; Gal 3:29).

Face To Face

While we are in the wilderness, Yah judges us "face to face." "For now, we see in a mirror dimly, but *then* face to face..." As we begin to see, we are "transformed" into Messiah's image. But to do this, we must first have a heart that willingly says, "Thy face, O Lord, I shall seek."[62] Such dedication helps us to see more clearly. Looking intently into the face of our Master helps us become more intimate with Him. Yeshua is the Word Incarnate and to intently study the Word is to look into His face— it is truly a form of worship. YHVH said He "will go away from us, and will return to His place, until we acknowledge our guilt, and seek His face." He also said of Israel, "In their affliction they will earnestly seek Me" (Hos 5:15).

Abba wants us to earnestly deal with our "guilt," for when we are repentant and seek His face, it produces a certain glory in us. Momentary light affliction produces an eternal glory. Godly sorrow brings repentance that leads to salvation. It produces, and makes us ready to see, justice done. Testing of our faith develops perseverance. And perseverance must finish its work, so we can mature and be complete, not lacking anything. [63]

Testing matures us. Affliction produces glory.

---

62 1 Cor 13:12; 2 Cor 3:18; Psa 27:8.
63 2 Cor 4:17; 7:10-11; Jas 1:3-4. Also, 1 Cor 10:13; 1 Pet 1:7; 4:19; Jas 1:3-4.

The Holy One said of this wasteland appointment: "I shall make you pass under the rod, and I shall bring you into the bond of the covenant." *Soncino Books of the Bible* says of the verse: "In separating the tithe of the herd or flock, it was the practice to make the animals pass one by one under the rod, and the tenth was separated and declared holy (cf. Lev 27:32). Similarly... before their deliverance from exile, [Israel] will be scrutinized by their Shepherd; the wicked will perish and the righteous will be saved." [64]

Like lambs destined for the altar, so Israel too, will be scrutinized— they will have to pass single-file under the rod of the Shepherd. There, He will separate the covenant keepers from the heathen:

> "I shall purge from you the rebels and those who transgress against Me; I shall bring them out of the land where they sojourn, but they will not enter the land ....For, the remnant of Israel will do no wrong and tell no lies, nor will a deceitful tongue be found in their mouths... They will no longer defile themselves with their idols, or with their detestable things, or with any of their transgressions; but I will deliver them from all their dwelling places in which they have sinned, and will cleanse them... All the sinners of My people will die by the sword, those who say, 'The calamity will not overtake or confront us'" (Lev 27:32; Jer 33:13; Eze 20:38; 37:23; Zep 3:13; Amos 9:10).

In the desert, Israel lacked water, and YHVH is the water they needed. He said, "My people have forsaken Me, the fountain of living waters, to hew for themselves cisterns, broken cisterns, that can hold no water" (Jer 2:13). Messiah Yeshua gives us Living Water. True faith in Him provides us with an unending supply (John 7:38).

---

[64] *Soncino Books of the Bible, Ezekiel* 20:37 comment, page 129.

KOL BA'MIDBAR

Because we need to come to this place for our own good, YHVH says of Israel, "I will allure her, and bring her into the wilderness" (Hos 2:14).

When He said this, He was speaking especially of those of Ephraim Israel. [65] One sin that He especially wants Ephraim to acknowledge at this time is: "Though I wrote for him ten thousand precepts of My law, they are regarded as a strange thing" (Hos 2:14; 8:12).

The Ephraimites especially did not have regard for the Father's precepts. They especially wanted to be like the Gentiles— so He scattered them among the heathen. Yet, He promised that their children would "respond to *Jezreel*" (Hos 2:22). Scattered among the nations, like seed that is planted, they would, one day experience a second birth, thus making them reborn sons of Israel. [66]

RETURNING TO JERUSALEM

Today, many are responding to the Holy Spirit's call to "go up to Jerusalem." They are joining in Israel's annual Tabernacles celebration. Believers from around the world come to show support for the people of Judah.

We also see that Ephraim is beginning to leave behind those who gather people unto themselves. He is refusing to drink the muddied waters of uncaring shepherds. He instead looks for those who seek after the Father's heart and feed the flock on knowledge and understanding. He

---

[65] Ephraim says, "After I turned back, I repented; after I was instructed, and came to know myself, I smote on my thigh; I was ashamed, humiliated, because I bore the reproach of my youth" (Jer 31:18-19). The sin of his youth is that he refused the Father's yoke and preferred the ways of the heathen (Hos 10:11).

[66] Alfred Edersheim, in his study of Rabbinical thought regarding the lost tribes, concludes: "As regards the ten tribes there is this truth underlying...that, as their persistent apostasy from the God of Israel and His worship had cut them off from His people, so the fulfillment of the Divine promises to them in the latter days would imply, as it were a second birth to make them once more Israel." See *Life and Times of Jesus the Messiah*, 1973, Eerdman's, pp 14-16.

is drinking of the "living water" that flows from Yeshua, the Shepherd King (Eze 34; Jer 3:15).

Although King Jeroboam long-ago created his own feast days and tried to change the set times, today's Ephraimites are repenting of the paganism of their forefathers. They are instead learning to celebrate anew the Father's Sabbath. They are learning to rejoice in His feasts in new and meaningful ways that speak of Messiah— and of Israel's full restoration (Lev 23:44; 1 Ki 12:32; Isa 42:21). [67]

Betrothed in the Wilderness

The Father said especially of latter-day Ephraim,

> "I will allure her, bring her into the wilderness and speak kindly to her. Then I will give her vineyards from there, and the valley of Achor as a door of hope. And she will sing there as in the days of her youth, as in the day when she came up from the land of Egypt." And, "You will call Me Ishi and will no longer call Me Baali. For I will remove the names of the Baals from her mouth, so that they will be mentioned by their names no more" (Hos 2:14-17).

Again, the Hebrew word, *midbar*, comes from *dbr*, which means *word*. Thus we see that *desert* is rooted in a word that means to speak, answer, commune, declare, talk, teach, and tell. In the wilderness the Father *speaks* to us. In the desert, we learn to *commune* with him. There, He *teaches* us His ways; we learn to hear the *word* of YHVH Elohim; we hear *Kol ba'Midbar*, the *Voice in the Wilderness*— the voice of the Holy One. [68] In the wilderness, formerly wayward ones are brought to a place of intimacy with the One they are to one day wed— and they *answer* His intimate call!

---

[67] See *Israel's Feasts and their Fullness: Expanded Edition*, Wootten.
Thanks to Hebrew Editor, and friend, Rimona Frank for the "DBR" insights.
[68] *S&BDB* # H4057 and 1696.

In the desert, Israel's children learn of the love the God of Israel has for them as individuals. They also learn faithfulness, and they learn to call the One they once called "Master," their "Husband." In this place of closing off, they become devoted to Him alone. They have eyes for no other. The fear of men is removed from before their face. They are driven with desire to be with their Beloved King. Thus they grow and blossom as "Betrothed Virgin Israel."

At Shavuot's initial fulfillment, the children of Israel stood in the desert at the foot of Mt. Horeb, and YHVH offered them His Covenant— which can be likened to a "Marriage Contract," a *Ketubah*. To Him, Israel in essence said, *"I do. I will keep your covenant."*

But instead, Israel did not listen to His voice...

Now, here we stand, children of Israel who are being given opportunity to learn to listen to His voice, to walk in His Wedding Covenant, and to know Him intimately, as our Husband and Maker. We must now *mean* and say to Him, *"I do. I will keep your covenant."*

Our Messiah, who is the Bridegroom, has given us His Spirit as a pledge. According to Scripture, this giving of the Holy Spirit is a "deposit" of things yet to come: "Now He who establishes us with you in Messiah and anointed us is God, who also sealed us and gave us the Spirit in our hearts as a pledge" (Rom 8:23; 2 Cor 1:21-22; 5:5; Eph 1:14; 2 Tim 1:14).

In our mortal bodies we are in a temporary tent (tabernacle), and "we groan, being burdened, because we do not want to be unclothed but to be clothed, so that what is mortal will be swallowed up." We also know that "He who prepared us for this very purpose is God, who gave to us the Spirit as a pledge." The Holy Spirit is part of our betrothal contract, so to speak, which seals the deal until its final consummation— at the Marriage Supper of the Lamb.

May we be so blessed as to sit at that glory-filled table!

The Voice... Hearing the Almighty

A Door of Hope

During our time in the desert, YHVH gives His chosen ones "the valley of Achor as a door of hope" (Hos 2:15). *Achor* means trouble; and after a season of it, Israel is restored. [69] At Achor, Achan and his conspirator family were stoned to death for dishonesty. His wicked actions brought curses and defeat to all Israel. Victory was withheld until Israel collectively dealt with their sin.

This event is said to be key to Israel's ultimate triumph as a people (Josh 7:24-26; Isa 65:10). Similarly, dealing with sin in our camp will prove to be key to our victory. It was true at Achor, and it is true today: The Kingdom of Israel will not be restored among thieves. We may lower our standards, and being deluded, think we are acceptable to our Maker, but we will not be judged based on standards we have contrived. We will be judged by His standards.

Feasting On Our Inheritance

We need to ask the Spirit to help us walk uprightly, so we can help repair the breach in Israel's broken brotherhood. We need His help to be able to break every yoke, so Israel can be set free. We need His help in order to raise up the age-old foundations. Then we will be called a repairer of the breach, a restorer of the streets in which to dwell.

As we learn to call the Sabbath a delight, and to delight in YHVH, He "will make us ride on the heights of the earth; and He will feed us with the heritage of Jacob our father" (Isa 58:1-14; Heb 4:1,9).

As beloved children of Israel, we are invited to a glorious wedding feast— but to sit at the Master's table we must be properly dressed for the occasion.

---

[69] S&BDB # H5911; Deu 8:2. See the book, *A Door of Hope for the Last Days* by Batya Ruth Wootten, 2009-10, Key of David Publishing, Saint Cloud, FL.

Festal Wedding Garments

In the Book of Matthew, Messiah Yeshua likens the kingdom of heaven to a story about a king who gave a wedding feast for his son. In this parable, the king sent out his slaves to call those who had been invited to the wedding, but they were unwilling to come. He did this a second time, and some even seized the king's slaves and mistreated and killed them. Then the king was enraged and sent his armies and destroyed those murderers and set their city on fire. He then said to his slaves, "The wedding is ready, but those who were invited were not worthy. Go therefore to the main highways, and as many as you find there, invite to the wedding feast."

The slaves gathered as many as they could, both evil and good; and the wedding hall was filled with guests. But, when the king came in to look them over, he saw a man there who was not dressed in wedding clothes, and he said to him, "Friend, how did you come in here without wedding clothes?" And the man was speechless.

So the king said to the servants, "Bind him hand and foot, and throw him into the outer darkness; in that place there will be weeping and gnashing of teeth. For many are called, but few are chosen" (Mat 22:1-14)

This parable reveals that, there are people who know about the wedding time and place, but perhaps have not met the Bridegroom face to face. At the very least, they have not followed His instructions. They did not buy from Him white garments with which to clothe themselves. They were not zealous about repenting (Rev 3:18-19).

While there is still time, we must buy from the Messiah, without cost, white wedding garments.

Regardless of what we may or may not know about the coming wedding feast, we simply will not be seated at His table without being clothed in His Righteousness.

We must now discard our sin-stained rags and ask the Holy Spirit to clothe us. We need to change into the change that Messiah now wants to bring forth in the earth.

It is time for us to realize that Messiah Yeshua wants to do a new thing in and through us. [70]

To accomplish His desire, we follow Yah's instructions: "Look to Abraham your father and to Sarah who gave birth to you in pain; when he was but one I called him, then I blessed him and multiplied him" (Isa 51:2).

Let us repent and seek to become the nation our Father wants us to be. Let us realize that Yah has decreed that, "Through this Jacob's iniquity will be forgiven; this will be the full price of the pardoning of his sin: when he makes all the altar stones like pulverized chalk stones; when Asherim and incense altars will not stand" (Isa 27:9). Let us learn to feed on the heritage of Jacob. Let us learn to walk in the simple, life-changing faith of our forefather Abraham. Let us learn to clearly hear the voice of our Beloved.

---

[70] Lam 3:22-23; Jer 31:22; Rev 2:17.

Sixteen

WHISPERS AND SHOUTS

Has the gentle voice of the Holy One spoken to us, and we have not yet obeyed? Has He tried to speak to us again and again, yet we have failed to respond?

If we repeatedly speak to someone and they do not respond to us, we stop talking. If so, then each of us needs to honestly ask our self the following questions:

Does the Almighty appear to be silent in my life? Am I in a place where I am no longer hearing His voice? Did I ignore His request the last time He spoke to me and tried to direct me?

If we respond in the affirmative to any of these questions, we must repent and go back to our point of departure from Abba's chosen path for us. We must not make excuses about our behavior, we must instead sincerely and openly declare that we are sorry. We must then ask the Father to once more speak to us by His Spirit, and we must seek to obey His every command. His required order is that we first show forth the fruit of repentance and then the fruit of obedience.

Remember, we serve a God who only had eight people

in the boat when He flooded everything. He is serious about having us repent of our sins. When He punishes, we get our punishment, and if we do not repent, we get a seven-fold punishment. [71]

Whispers in the Ear— Shouts From the Housetops

Messiah Yeshua said to His followers, "What I tell you in the darkness, speak in the light; and what you hear whispered in your ear, proclaim upon the housetops."

The truth is that YHVH sometimes whispers things in our ear that we are afraid to even mention to others. That is why Yeshua warned us about the sin of fearing men: "Do not fear those who kill the body but are unable to kill the soul; but rather fear Him who is able to destroy both soul and body in hell" (Mat 10:27-28).

Sometimes we hear the voice of our Messiah whispering mysteries in our ear, yet our fear of man keeps us from speaking aloud Yeshua's liberating truths.

---

[71] In Leviticus we see the principle that, if the Almighty seeks to correct us and we do not turn from our sinful ways and begin to obey Him, He will then punish us "sevenfold" for our sins (Lev 26:18, 27-28). In Ezekiel we see that both Ephraim and Judah were given certain punishments for their idolatry. And, in addition to her 40 years, Judah also had to "drink her sister's cup" for an additional 390-year penalty. This gave Judah a total of 430 years of punishment, which began when their capital, Jerusalem, became a vassal city of Babylon. Judah lost political control around 595 B.C., and their punishment came to an end in 166 B.C., when the Temple was cleansed by the Maccabees. However, Ephraim did not repent of her idolatries, so her 390-year punishment was increased sevenfold, resulting in a total of 2730 years in which she would be "Not a people" (Hosea 1-2). Her cities became vassals of conquering Assyria starting in 734 B.C. She lost her capital, Samaria, and went into captivity in 722 B.C. If we use the prophetic, 360 day calendar, we see the 2730 years ended around 1967, the year Jerusalem was reclaimed as modern Israel's capital (see Gen 7:11,24; 8:3-4; 5-14; Rev 11:2-3; 12:6,14; 13:5). If we use a solar calendar, we see the punishment ending around 1996, and no later than 2008. In our day Ephraim continues to be restored to her Israelite roots and heritage. (See *Restoring Israel's Kingdom* by Angus Wootten, 2000, Key of David Publishing, Saint Cloud, FL, p 131.)

While we need to know when to quietly ponder things in our heart, as did Mary, the mother of our Messiah, we also must beware not speaking up for fear of man.

We need to speak aloud the precious truths the Holy One graciously imparts to us. He does not reveal His secret things so we will keep them hidden from others. He reveals His truths to us so we can share them as He leads.

Daring to Be Different

Simon the Tanner lived by the Mediterranean Sea, and during a visit to his house, Peter the Apostle went up to Simon's rooftop to pray. Hungry and waiting for the noon meal to be prepared, Peter fell into a trance. But the vision he saw seemed to go against all that his fathers had taught him. Peter saw heaven opened and a large sheet being lowered down to earth that contained all kinds of unclean animals, reptiles, birds, and crawling things.

Then, a voice out of Heaven spoke to him:

"Arise, Peter. Kill and eat."

"Surely not, Lord!" Peter replied. "I have never eaten anything impure or unclean."

Three times this happened. Then the voice came again: "Simon, three men are looking for you. Go downstairs and do not hesitate to go with them for I have sent them."

Simon Peter ultimately did the unthinkable for a Jewish man— he invited "unclean Gentiles" into Simon's house to be his guests at the table.

Why?

Because Peter understood the vision God gave him: "God has shown me that I should not call any *man* unclean" he said (Acts 10:9-48).

Peter dared to be different. He dared to believe the voice from Heaven, and he will forever be blessed for it.

We need to do the same.

The Voice... Hearing the Almighty

Paul likewise heard the voice of the Almighty. In this case, the voice and the light of its revelation literally knocked Paul off his horse. Then the voice began to teach Paul things that differed radically from the human voices Paul had previously listened to.

Paul nonetheless dared to believe and to act on the truth he was given. Later called "Paul, an Apostle," or *Sent One*, he was greatly used by the Father to change the world. This happened because Paul chose to respond to the voice of the Almighty.

Truly Hearing His Voice

When we seek to hear and obey the Father's voice, we must realize that, if we think it is His voice, but in truth it is not, and if we follow the wrong voice, we will reap the consequences. We cannot simply move out based on our own assumptions, and then, when everything falls apart around us, ask Abba to bless our mess.

On the other hand, we can trust that He will always be with us as we seek to clean up our lives.

Because there are consequences to sin (sin means to miss the mark), we want to be certain that the voice we listen to belongs to YHVH. To be sure that it is His voice and not ours, or the voice of the evil one, we turn to YHVH's Word. In its inspired pages we can always find a second witness. Because we belong to Messiah, we can come boldly into His throne room of grace to inquire of Him. And we can trust that His voice will *never* contradict His Holy Word or go against His commandments. [72] It is our duty to search the Word to make sure the things we think we are hearing are affirmed in its pages: "Study to show thyself approved unto God, a workman that needeth not to be ashamed, rightly dividing the word of truth (2 Tim 2:15, KJV).

---

[72] Deu 13:18; 15:5; 26:17; 30:20.

Reaching Into His World...

The Father says to us, "Obey My voice, and I will be your God, and you will be My people; and you will walk in all the way which I command you, that it may be well with you" (Jer 7:23).

Again we note that sometimes Abba seems to be silent. He does not seem to be as active in our lives as when we were babes in Messiah. Sometimes we do not seem to hear His voice as often as we did when we were new Believers.

This is possibly so because, when we are babes, the Father often reaches into our world and gently touches us. During these times, He is ever wooing us, ever caring for and encouraging us as we take our first baby steps in the faith. But, as we mature, He sometimes seems to get quiet, and not reaching out to us as in times past. The reason for this is, because of His great love for us, He is trying to get us to seek Him— because He wants us to grow up and learn to reach into *His world*. [73]

Times of silence can actually be times of true growth and maturation. As we mature, we learn to, even long to, reach into our Father's world. If our world seems silent, it is time to reach out to our Heavenly Father.

Repentance Without Regret...

In times of apparent silence, Abba can also be teaching us a different principle. Sometimes He is silent because He does not want to turn us into puppets. He is not looking for robots, but for those who will love Him of their own free will and choose to serve Him. So, He sometimes wants us to learn things for ourselves. He appears to us to be silent at these times. But rest assured that He is ever the "Refiner" who is carefully watching over us (Mal 3:3).

---

[73] Thanks to Graham Cooke for this excellent point: www.grahamcooke.com

The Voice... Hearing the Almighty

There are times when we seem to have no choice but to make a choice in a given situation. Sometimes, such choices turn out well, and we are encouraged in our ability to make right choices. But at other times, our decisions result in what we might call "mistakes." However, in Abba's economy they may not be mistakes at all...

Paul said to the Corinthians:

> "I now rejoice, not that you were made sorrowful, but that you were made sorrowful to the point of repentance; for you were made sorrowful according to the will of God, so that you might not suffer loss in anything.... For the sorrow that is according to the will of God produces a repentance without regret, leading to salvation, but the sorrow of the world produces death" (2 Cor 7:9-10).

Worldly sorrow produces death. But Godly sorrow produces "repentance without regret." Repentance that leaves no regrets seems to be an oxymoron, opposites that do not go together. Yet, in the economy of the Holy One, the two add up to perfect repentance: We are sorry for our actions, but we learned valuable lessons from the experience. This, in turn, brought positive changes in us, and that makes it hard for us to "regret" having chosen the path that we chose, even though it was a wrong path.

Due to our own previous choices, we had to go down that particular path— because we had to learn a certain lesson. In turn, our choice led us to a "godly sorrow"— which produced good in us. And in true Hebraic form, more so than *what* we are being turned away from, our focus is on *whom* we are turning toward, the Holy One. In the end, our "mistake" led us into a deeper relationship with Him, and thus hardly qualifies as a true "mistake." [74]

---

[74] For more information on this subject, see *Israel's Feasts and their Fullness*: (continued...)

Whatever method Abba may choose to use to speak to us, if we will but be still and listen, then obey Him, we will be drawn into a deep and intimate relationship of love with Him. We will be His child and He will be our God.

To learn to walk in this way, to be empowered to grow up in Messiah, we would do well to say the following prayer. If need be, we can say it often, and we should always say it with heart-felt conviction:

Abba, please save me from mistaken people.
Protect me and do not allow me to be deceived by anyone.
I truly want to be empowered to hear Your voice.

I do not want to think I am hearing Your voice, but truly want to hear from You. Therefore, Abba, I ask that, You would also mercifully save me from myself and from my own deceptions.

Please do not allow my own heart to deceive me. Instead, give me ears to hear You alone, and please give me a heart that simply will not follow another.

Empower me, Father. Fill me now with Your Holy Spirit.
In Messiah Yeshua's Name I pray.
Amen.

---

74 (...continued)
Expanded Edition, Batya Ruth Wootten, Chapter 31, "Repentance and Returning – Tashlich and Teshuvah," 2008, Key of David Publishing, Saint Cloud, FL.

The Voice... Hearing the Almighty

SEVENTEEN

The Road to Zion...

Two of Messiah Yeshua's disciples were on the Road to Emmaus, a village located about seven miles from Jerusalem. They were talking with each other about the many things that had taken place concerning Yeshua's crucifixion.

While they were discussing the matters, Yeshua Himself approached and began traveling with them. But their eyes were prevented from recognizing Him. Then He said to them, "What are these words that you are exchanging with one another as you are walking?"

They stood still, looking very sad. One of them, named Cleopas, answered and said to Him, "Are You the only one visiting Jerusalem and unaware of the things which have happened here in these days?"

And Yeshua said to them, "What things?"

They answered Him, "The things about Yeshua the Nazarene, who was a prophet mighty in deed and word in the sight of YHVH Elohim and all the people, and how the chief priests and our rulers delivered Him to the sentence of death, and crucified Him. We were hoping that it was He who was going to redeem Israel. Indeed, besides all this, it is the third day since these things happened. Also some women among us amazed us. When they were at the tomb early in the morning, and did not find His body, they came, saying that they had also seen a vision of angels who said that He was alive. Some of those who were with us went to the tomb and found it just exactly as the women also had said; but Him they did not see."

So Yeshua said to them, "O foolish men and slow of heart to believe in all that the prophets have spoken! Was it not necessary for the Messiah to suffer these things and to enter into His glory?"

Then, beginning with Moses and all the prophets, Messiah Yeshua explained to them the things concerning Himself in all the Scriptures (see Luke 24-13-27).

In this account, we see a prophetic picture that has to do with the times in which we live. In many ways, these disciples who loved the Messiah, yet could not see Him for the truth of Who He was, depict some in our movement.

- The disciples were close to Jerusalem:
  So are we. We are surely approaching the time when Messiah Yeshua will return and forevermore establish His Eternal Kingdom, and it will be established in the City of the Great King: New Jerusalem (Psa 48:2; Mat 5:35).
- These disciples did not recognize their Redeemer:
  Some in our movement do not recognize Yeshua for who He is, which is the Great I AM. Scripture reveals that unbelievers picked up stones to stone Him *because* they felt He, "being a man, made Himself out to be God"— and because He said of Himself, "Truly, truly, I say to you, before Abraham was born, I AM." Yeshua is the Word Incarnate, He is God/Elohim in the flesh (John 1:1-4; 8:59; 10:33).

- The words of the disciples were not accurate. They saw that Yeshua was "a *prophet* mighty in deed" but were discouraged in that He had been put to death. They only saw Him as a man, a prophet:
  Some in our movement mistakenly see Yeshua in this same way, which is sad. They too need to have their eyes opened that they might truly see Him.
- The disciples did not know the full truth about the Resurrected Messiah. They did not see Him as God Incarnate who would overcome sin and death (Rom 8:2; 1 Cor 15:56-57; Rev 3:21).
  Some in our movement too, need to have these things clarified for them, so their joy will be full.
- They hoped Yeshua would "redeem" Israel:
  They wanted political redemption, but Yeshua's kingdom is not of this world (John 8:23; 18:36). They did not comprehend YHVH's plan of redemption— which begins with being saved from the eternal grave— and only Elohim can be that kind of Redeemer. "No man can by any means redeem his brother or give to God a ransom for him— For the redemption of his soul is costly, And he should cease trying forever— But God/Elohim will redeem my soul from the power of Sheol, He will receive me" (Psa 49:7-8,15).
- The disciples did not accurately see Yeshua in Scripture. So, He had to explain Torah to them:
  Some in our movement mistakenly speak against the validity of the New Covenant Scriptures. They think they understand Torah but do not see that it tells of a Prophet like Moses and that the Father promised to put "His Words" in that Prophet's mouth. Yeshua is that Prophet, and the New Covenant contains those Torah promised Words (Deu 18:18-19; John 5:46; 8:28; 12:49-50; 17:8,17).

The Voice... Hearing the Almighty

The prophetic picture that is painted in this account is this: if we do not understand that Messiah Yeshua is the I AM come in the flesh to redeem us but first had to suffer for our sins, we do not really understand Torah. Yeshua said of Himself, "If you believed Moses, you would believe Me, for he wrote about Me. But if you do not believe his writings, how will you believe My words?" (John 5:46-47).

We must learn to see our Messiah in the written Torah, for He is the Living Torah, He is true Torah come alive!

The Road to Zion...

If we want to travel the Road to Zion, we must first embrace the full truth about our Messiah.

On that road of promise, in Him, we become "One stick in our Father's hand," even as is prophesied by Ezekiel (chapter 37). When we travel that road, and Judah and Ephraim walk as one, we see King David's restored booth. We also will not fear any marauders because Judah will be like a bow and Ephraim its flaming arrow. Most importantly, we know that YHVH *Tsava'ot*, the LORD of Hosts, will defend us from all enemies. He will make us like stones of a crown that sparkle in His Holy Land. We also know that He will strengthen Judah and save Joseph. And that, at that time, Judah will be like a majestic horse in battle, and Ephraim will be like a mighty man, their heart glad as if from wine, their children glad with them.

Yes, YHVH will soon whistle for them to gather them together, and they will return, they will come until no more room can be found for them (Zech 9:13-10:10).

Our God long-ago promised that He would restore the once divided house of Israel. He promised to save the house of Judah and the house of Israel from the east and the west. And at that time, Judah and Ephraim will call Zion "The City of Truth" (Zec 8:3,7,13).

The Road to Zion...

We want to begin our walk toward that promised City. However, to be fully restored, we must walk in sinlessness. Isaiah 27:9 says, "Through this Jacob's iniquity will be forgiven; this will be the full price of the pardoning of his sin: when he makes all the altar stones like pulverized chalk stones; when Asherim and incense altars will not stand."

To be truly repentant, learn to feed on the heritage of Jacob, and walk in the simple, life-changing faith of our forefather Abraham, is our call. We need to walk in these things now. Jeremiah foretold a day when "the sons of Israel will come, both they and the sons of Judah as well; they will go along weeping as they go, and it will be YHVH their God that they seek. They will ask for the way to Zion, turning their faces in its direction; they will come that they may join themselves to YHVH in an everlasting covenant." And, "At that time...search will be made for the iniquity of Israel, but there will be none; and for the sins of Judah, but they will not be found" (Jer 50:4-5,20).

The Holy One has sworn: "All the sinners of my people will die by the sword. ... I will cut off all idols...and unclean spirits. ...I will also remove from your midst your proud, exulting ones. And you will never again be haughty on My holy mountain. I will leave among you a humble and lowly people, and they will take refuge in the name of YHVH. The remnant of Israel will do no wrong and tell no lies, nor will a deceitful tongue be found in their mouths" (Amos 9:10; Zec 13:2; Zep 3:11-13).

At that time, Ephraim and Judah will call Jerusalem, "The Throne of YHVH, and will no more walk after the stubbornness of their evil heart."

"In those days the house of Judah will walk with the house of Israel, and they will come together from the land of the north" (Jer 3:14-18).

In the Last Days, Reunited Israel will be empowered from on High!

The Voice... Hearing the Almighty

Redeemed Israel will no longer be stiff-necked and resist the Ruach but will instead constantly look to the Holy Spirit to guide and confirm to them the will of the Holy One of Israel.

Restored Israel will preach true Torah. At that time, the eternal, life-giving, compassionate, loving instructions of the Holy One of Israel will in truth be forever written on their hearts.

May we become that redeemed, reunited and restored people whose feet are firmly planted on the Glorious Road to Zion!
May our journey begin right now— in this moment.
Father, we humbly ask you to please speak to our heart.
We want to hear Your voice, Father God.
We want to follow You, and You alone.
Amen! So be it!

Eighteen

Ha Kol Shel Abba

In the latter days you will return to YHVH your God and listen to His voice (Deu 4:30).

HaKol Shel Abba means, *The Voice of the Father (Daddy)*.

As stated in the beginning, our Father wants us to learn to once more hear, within ourselves, His comforting voice. It is His desire that we return to the precious position we once held in *Gan Eden*, the Garden of Eden.

In closing, we ask that you allow the words of the following song to minister to your spirit.

HaKol Shel Abba
The voice of the Father
HaKol Shel Abba
Have you heard it?

HaKol Shel Abba
HaKol Shel Abba
Shema Yisrael
HaKol Shel Abba

The Voice... Hearing the Almighty

In Gan Eden
Your voice was within
In Gan Eden
Your voice was within
But we let sin enter in
We let sin enter in

We heard Your voice in the Garden
Knew we needed pardon
Knew a price had to be paid
So we hid and were afraid
O, Forgive us our sin
Abba, let us return to Gan Eden

HaKol Shel Abba
HaKol Shel Abba
Shema Yisrael
HaKol Shel Abba...

In closing, we pray:

Precious Father,
We now realize how important it is for us to learn to hear Your voice. We realize how vital it is to our well-being that we learn to listen to You.
Please lead and guide us in Your way.
Give us ears to hear and a heart to obey You.
We love You, Abba and ask that you fill us with Your Spirit.
We trust in You and look forward to the many good things You have planned for our lives.
In Messiah Yeshua's Name we pray.
Amen and Amen.

Study Helps

Study Helps

The following charts, maps, and lists are presented to help the student better understand "both the houses of Israel" (Isa 8:14).

The Divided Kingdom: Israel and Judah

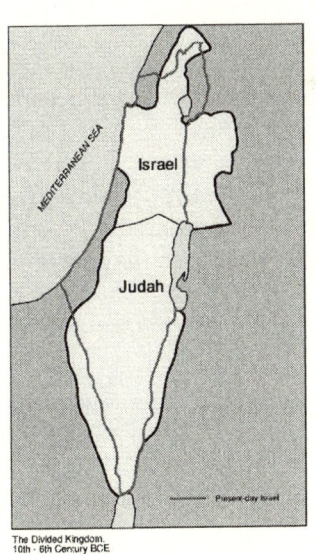

The Divided Kingdom,
10th - 6th Century BCE

THE VOICE... HEARING THE ALMIGHTY

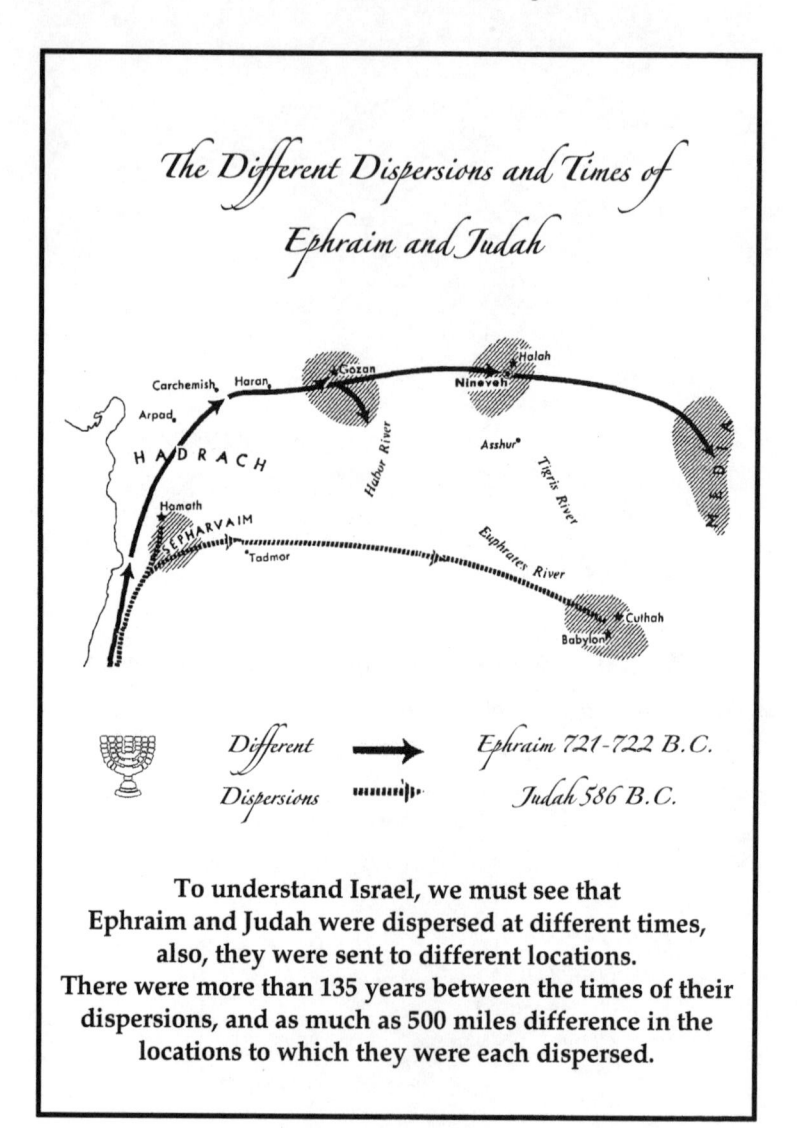

The Different Dispersions and Times of Ephraim and Judah

Different Dispersions → *Ephraim 721-722 B.C.*
Judah 586 B.C.

To understand Israel, we must see that
Ephraim and Judah were dispersed at different times,
also, they were sent to different locations.
There were more than 135 years between the times of their
dispersions, and as much as 500 miles difference in the
locations to which they were each dispersed.

From the book, *Redeemed Israel: Reunited and Restored*
by Batya Ruth Wootten.

Study Helps

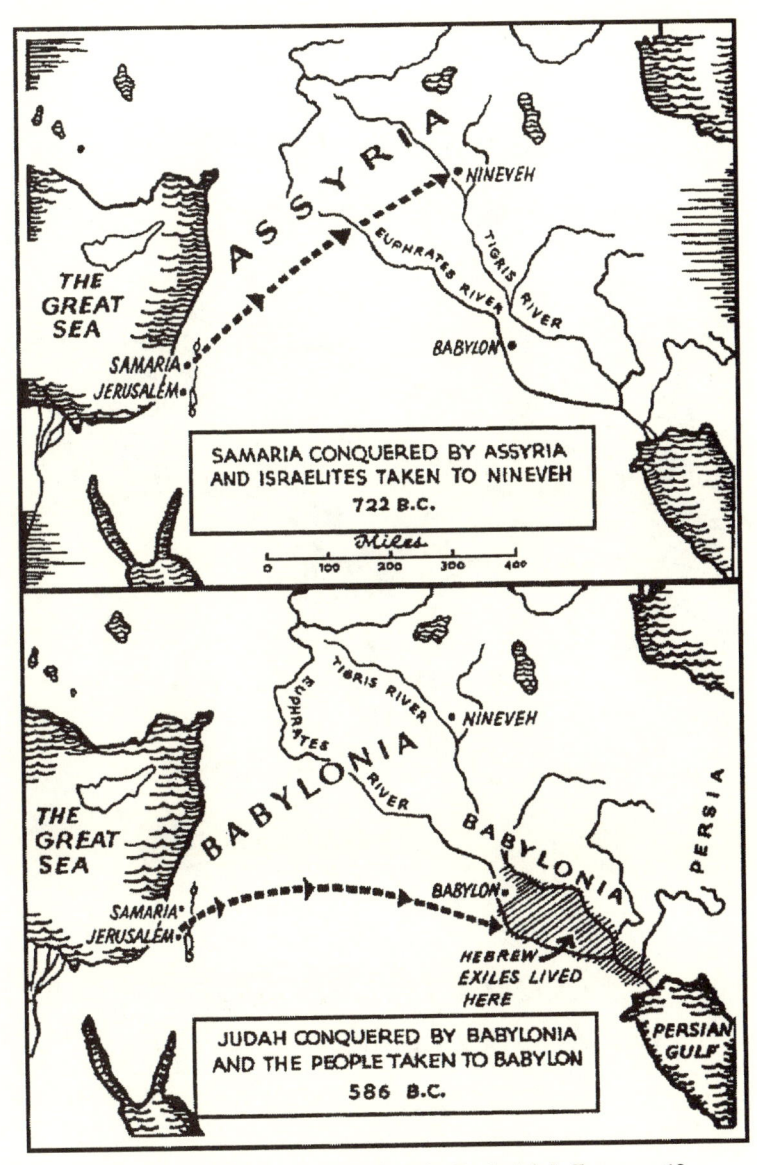

SAMARIA CONQUERED BY ASSYRIA
AND ISRAELITES TAKEN TO NINEVEH
722 B.C.

JUDAH CONQUERED BY BABYLONIA
AND THE PEOPLE TAKEN TO BABYLON
586 B.C.

From *A Map Book For Bible Students* by Frederick L. Fay, page 18,
Old Tappan, NJ: Fleming H. Revell.
Used by permission.

The Voice... Hearing The Almighty

There Are Two Main Branches In The Olive Tree Of Israel: Ephraim And Judah

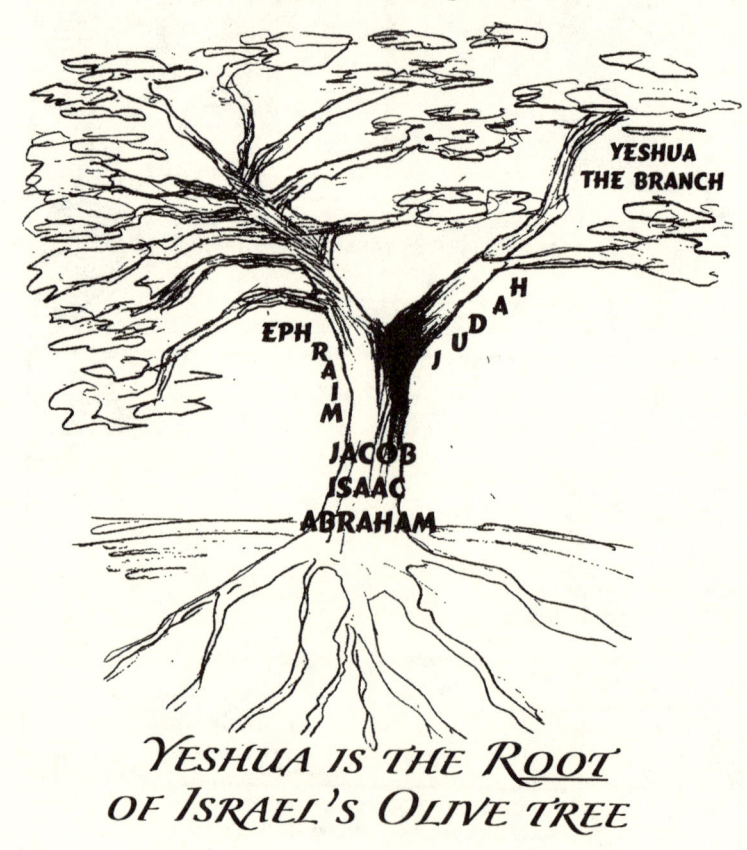

(Illustration of olive tree labeled: YESHUA THE BRANCH, EPHRAIM, JUDAH, JACOB, ISAAC, ABRAHAM)

Yeshua Is The Root Of Israel's Olive Tree

When the Father first called "Israel" an "olive tree,"
He specifically said He was speaking to
"the house of Israel and the house of Judah" (Jer 11:10).
Yeshua said, "I am the root and the offspring of David."
Isaiah calls the Messiah "the Branch"
(Rev 22:16; Isa 11:1).

STUDY HELPS

THE FIVE STAGES OF ISRAEL'S OLIVE TREE

1. Jeremiah's Olive Tree With both branches: Ephraim and Judah (Jer 11:10,16)

2. Ephraim's Branches Broken Off Dispersed among the Nations (722 B.C.)

3. Judah's Broken Branches Dispersed to Babylon (586 B.C.)

4. Paul's Olive Tree: 30 A.D. With some from Judah who returned from Babylon (Rom 11)

Israel's Restored Olive Tree "Both Branches" (*etz/sticks/branches/trees*) made one in the Father's Hand (Eze 37:15-28)

The Voice... Hearing the Almighty

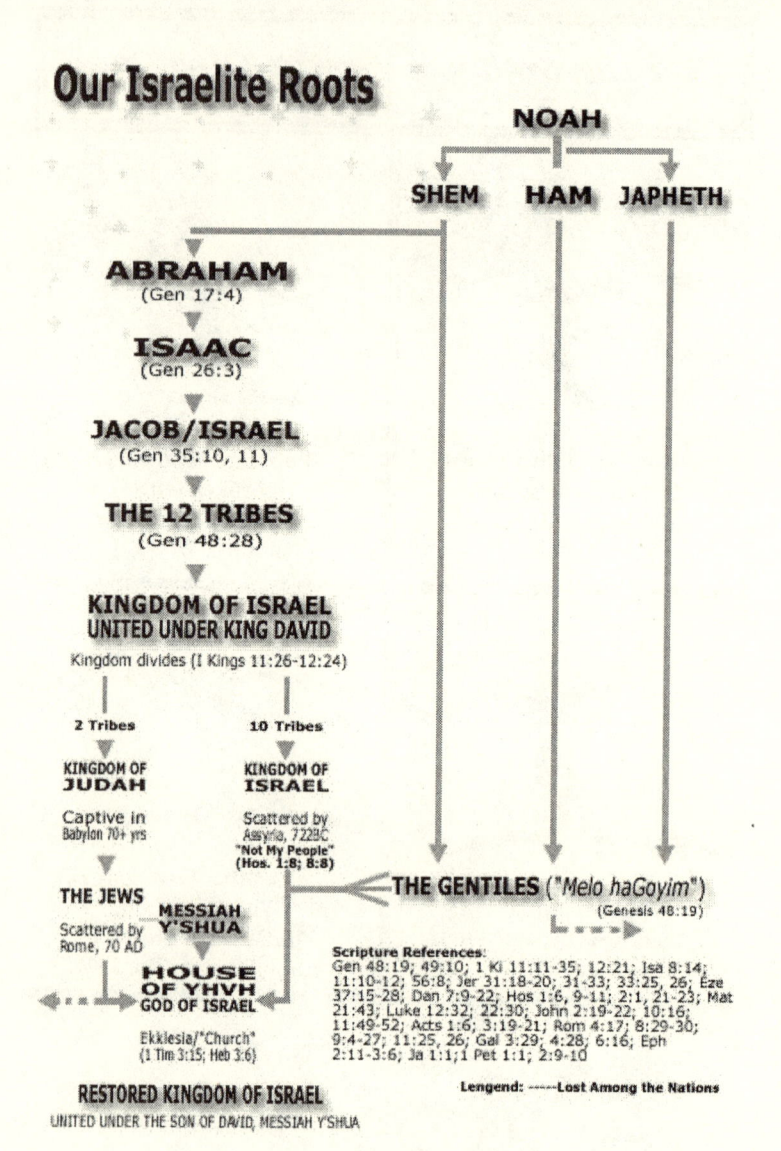

Our Israelite Roots

NOAH
├── **SHEM**
├── **HAM**
└── **JAPHETH**

ABRAHAM (Gen 17:4)
↓
ISAAC (Gen 26:3)
↓
JACOB/ISRAEL (Gen 35:10, 11)
↓
THE 12 TRIBES (Gen 48:28)
↓
KINGDOM OF ISRAEL — UNITED UNDER KING DAVID

Kingdom divides (I Kings 11:26-12:24)

2 Tribes → **KINGDOM OF JUDAH** — Captive in Babylon 70+ yrs → **THE JEWS** — Scattered by Rome, 70 AD

10 Tribes → **KINGDOM OF ISRAEL** — Scattered by Assyria, 722BC — "Not My People" (Hos. 1:8; 8:8) → **THE GENTILES** ("*Melo haGoyim*") (Genesis 48:19)

MESSIAH Y'SHUA

HOUSE OF YHVH — GOD OF ISRAEL

Ekklesia/"Church" (1 Tim 3:15; Heb 3:6)

RESTORED KINGDOM OF ISRAEL
UNITED UNDER THE SON OF DAVID, MESSIAH Y'SHUA

Scripture References:
Gen 48:19; 49:10; 1 Ki 11:11-35; 12:21; Isa 8:14; 11:10-12; 56:8; Jer 31:18-20; 31-33; 33:25, 26; Eze 37:15-28; Dan 7:9-22; Hos 1:6, 9-11; 2:1, 21-23; Mat 21:43; Luke 12:32; 22:30; John 2:19-22; 10:16; 11:49-52; Acts 1:6; 3:19-21; Rom 4:17; 8:29-30; 9:4-27; 11:25, 26; Gal 3:29; 4:28; 6:16; Eph 2:11-3:6; Ja 1:1; 1 Pet 1:1; 2:9-10

Legend: -----Lost Among the Nations

Study Helps

Scripture	Restored Israel Hallmarks
Isaiah 11:13	Ephraim's jealousy departs
Jeremiah 31:18,19	Ephraim repents of his paganism
Isaiah 11:13	Those hostile to Judah are cut off
Isaiah 11:13	Judah ceases to vex Ephraim
Zechariah 10:7	Ephraim becomes like a mighty man
Hosea 11:10	Ephraim comes trembling from the West
Zechariah 10:8,10	Ephraim returns in great numbers
Obadiah 1:18	Jacob becomes a fire, Joseph a flame
Zechariah 9:13	Judah is like a bow, Ephraim the arrow
Jeremiah 3:14; 50:5	Repentant Israel asks for the way to Zion
Jeremiah 50:20	No more iniquity found in Israel
Jeremiah 3:17; 16:14	Both forget the Ark and the Exodus
Zechariah 8:3,7,13	Both call Zion The City of Truth
Ezekiel 37:15-28	Two sticks become one nation in the land
Ezekiel 37:24	Ephraim & Judah have one King— Yeshua
Ezekiel 37:23-24	Not defiled with any transgressions
Ezekiel 37:26-27	YHVH's sanctuary is in their midst forever

Until the above verses are completely fulfilled
the Father is still working with both the houses of Israel.
Ephraim and Judah have not been fully reunited—
our unity has been imputed in the Messiah,
but we have not fully implemented that unity.
Copyright © Batya Ruth Wootten.

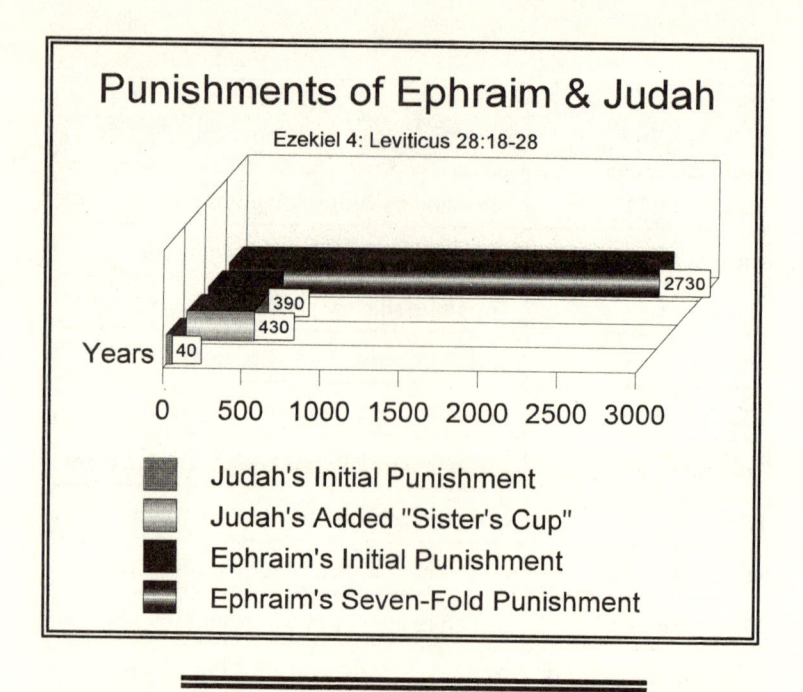

Punishments of Ephraim & Judah
Ezekiel 4: Leviticus 28:18-28

Years	
40	Judah's Initial Punishment
390	Ephraim's Initial Punishment
430	Judah's Added "Sister's Cup"
2730	Ephraim's Seven-Fold Punishment

In Ezekiel we see that both Ephraim and Judah were given certain punishments for their idiolatry. However, in addition to her 40 years, Judah also had to "drink her sister's cup" for an additional 390 year penalty. This gave Judah a total of 430 years of punishment, which began when their capital, Jerusalem, became a vassal city of Babylon. Judah lost their political control around 595 B.C. Their punishment came to an end in 166 B.C., with the cleansing of the Temple by the Maccabees.

On the other hand, Ephraim did not repent of her idolatries, so her 390 year punishment was increased sevenfold, resulting in a total of 2730 years in which she would be "Not a people," even as Hosea prophesied. Ephraim's cities slowly became vassal cities of conquering Assyria starting in 734 B.C. She lost her capital, Samaria, and went into captivity in 722 B.C. Thus, her "Not a people" punishment ended in 1996. She continues today to be restored to her Israelite roots and heritage.

For more information concerning these punishments, see the book, *Restoring Israel's Kingdom* by Angus Wootten, 2000, Key of David Publishing, Saint Cloud, FL.

STUDY HELPS

FALL AND RESTORATION OF ISRAEL'S KINGDOM

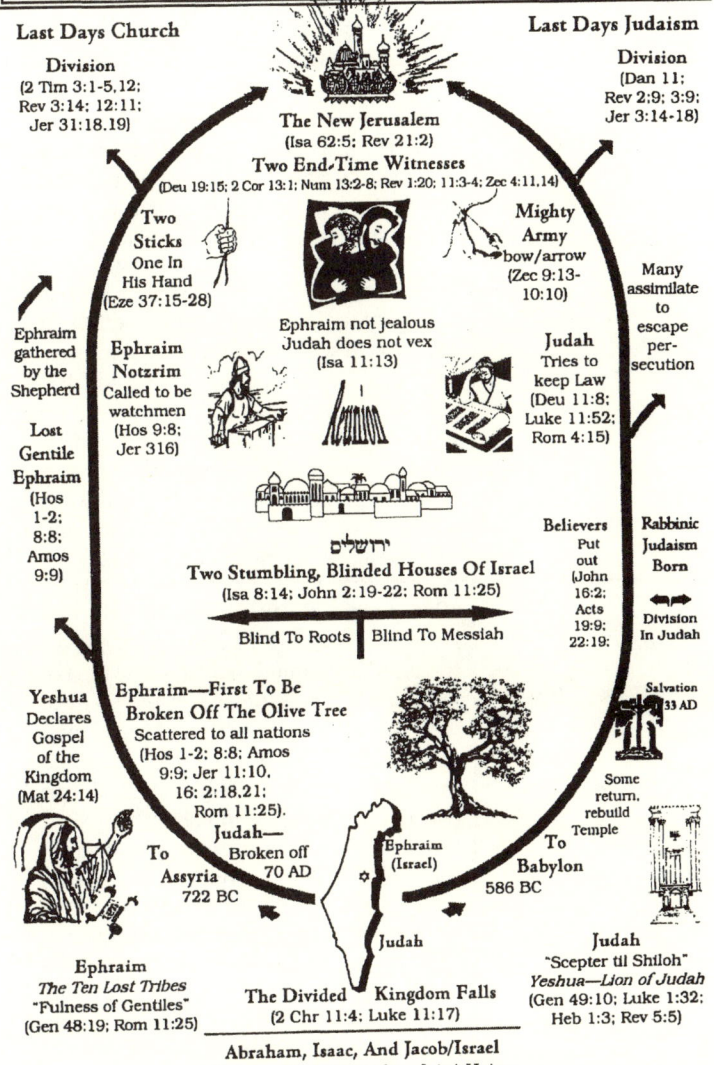

Last Days Church
Division
(2 Tim 3:1-5,12;
Rev 3:14; 12:11;
Jer 31:18,19)

Last Days Judaism
Division
(Dan 11;
Rev 2:9; 3:9;
Jer 3:14-18)

The New Jerusalem
(Isa 62:5; Rev 21:2)
Two End-Time Witnesses
(Deu 19:15; 2 Cor 13:1; Num 13:2-8; Rev 1:20; 11:3-4; Zec 4:11,14)

Two Sticks
One In His Hand
(Eze 37:15-28)

Mighty Army
bow/arrow
(Zec 9:13-10:10)

Many assimilate to escape persecution

Ephraim gathered by the Shepherd

Ephraim Notzrim
Called to be watchmen
(Hos 9:8; Jer 3:16)

Ephraim not jealous Judah does not vex
(Isa 11:13)

Judah Tries to keep Law
(Deu 11:8; Luke 11:52; Rom 4:15)

Lost Gentile Ephraim
(Hos 1-2; 8:8; Amos 9:9)

ירושלים

Two Stumbling, Blinded Houses Of Israel
(Isa 8:14; John 2:19-22; Rom 11:25)

Blind To Roots ← → Blind To Messiah

Believers Put out
(John 16:2; Acts 19:9; 22:19)

Rabbinic Judaism Born
Division In Judah

Yeshua Declares Gospel of the Kingdom
(Mat 24:14)

Ephraim—First To Be Broken Off The Olive Tree
Scattered to all nations
(Hos 1-2; 8:8; Amos 9:9; Jer 11:10, 16; 2:18,21; Rom 11:25).

Judah—Broken off 70 AD

Ephraim (Israel)

Judah

Salvation 33 AD

Some return, rebuild Temple

To Assyria 722 BC

To Babylon 586 BC

Judah
"Scepter til Shiloh"
Yeshua—Lion of Judah
(Gen 49:10; Luke 1:32; Heb 1:3; Rev 5:5)

Ephraim
The Ten Lost Tribes
"Fulness of Gentiles"
(Gen 48:19; Rom 11:25)

The Divided Kingdom Falls
(2 Chr 11:4; Luke 11:17)

Abraham, Isaac, And Jacob/Israel
Father of a Multitude—Joint Heirs
(Gen 26:3; 28:4; 1 Chr 16:16-17; Heb 11:9,39,40; Gal 3:29)

We Are Spirit, Soul, and Body

YOU ARE A SPIRIT **YOU HAVE A SOUL** **YOU LIVE IN A BODY**	"May the God of peace Himself sanctify you entirely; and may your **spirit** and **soul** and **body** be preserved complete, without blame at the coming of our Lord Messiah Yeshua" (1 Thes 5:23; also see Heb 4:12).
BODY	"I urge you, brethren, by the mercies of God, to present your **bodies** a living and holy sacrifice, acceptable to God, which is your spiritual service of worship. And do not be conformed to this world, but be transformed by the renewing of your **mind**, so that you may prove what the will of God is, that which is good and acceptable and perfect" (Rom 12:1-2).
SOUL: **INCLUDES MIND,** **WILL,** **EMOTIONS**	"Put aside all filthiness and all that remains of wickedness, in humility receive the word implanted, which is able to save your **souls**....be renewed in the spirit of your **mind**." ...[For] YHVH "formed man of dust from the ground, and breathed into his nostrils the breath of life; and man became a living **soul/being**." ... [So,] "watch over your **heart** with all diligence, for from it flow the springs of life" (James 1:21; Eph 4:23; Gen 2:7; Pro 4:23).
SPIRIT Chart idea by Paul Jablonowski: www.sonstoglory.com	"The lamp of the LORD searches the **spirit** of a man; it searches out his inmost being. ...You have come to...the general assembly and church of the firstborn who are enrolled in heaven, and to God, Judge of all, and to the **spirits** of the righteous made perfect" (Pro 20:27, NIV; Heb 12:22-23).

Hearing Aids

Tips to help us better hear our Father's voice:

We repent in Messiah's name, in word and deed. We ask Him to fill us with His Spirit.

We confirm *words* with *the Word* (Mal 3:6; Heb 13:8).

The Father's voice will sometimes be still and small, so we must always be carefully listening (1 Ki 19:11-13).

Yeshua said, from our "innermost being will flow rivers of living water." This speaks "of the Spirit." It tells us that the voice of the Spirit will rise up from our inner man. We want to be suspect of ideas that flow down from our carnal mind, because it often opposes the truths of our God (John 7:37-39; Rom 8:7).

We need to have our senses trained, which means we may make some "mistakes" along the way. We pray for the gift of discernment of spirits, yet we know that "mis-steps" are part of our development (Gen 50:20; 1 Cor 12:10; 2 Cor 7:9-10; Heb 4:13; 5:14).

While we want to talk to the Father in prayer, we also need to learn to listen to Him. To do this, we may have to wait on Him. And, we must surrender ourselves to Him completely (Psa 37:7; 62:5; Lam 3:25).

We guard our speech, knowing we will give an account for every word we speak. "By your words you will be justified, and by your words you will be condemned" (Mat 12:36-37).

We guard and treasure the awesome gift of being able to hear the Father's voice in our lives. And, we trust that, by His Spirit, He will lovingly guide and direct us in all our ways (Jer 29:11; Heb 11:6).

Glossary of Hebrew Words

- *Abba:* Affectionate term for Father, like Daddy.
- *Brit HaDoshah:* The New [Renewed] Covenant.
- *Gan Eden:* Garden of Eden
- *Messiah Yeshua:* Jesus was given the Hebrew name Yeshua when He was born. Christ is from the Greek *Christos*, which is translated from the Hebrew, *Moshiach:* From this word we get *Messiah*, which means anointed.
- *Mikvah:* Ritual bath in running water (such as the Jordan River). Baptism.
- *Mishnah:* Code of Jewish Oral Law
- *Moshiach:* Anointed One (see Messiah Yeshua)
- *Rav:* Shortened form of Rabbi
- *Ruach haKodesh: The Spirit Most Holy*
- *Shekhinah:* The visible divine Presence that rested between the cherubim over the Ark's Mercy Seat.
- *Taleet (Talit, Talis):* Prayer shawl with ceremonial fringe (see *Tzit-tzit*) on the four corners.
- *Tanach (Tenach):* Acronym for the Hebrew Bible, consisting of Torah, Prophets, and Writings; from the initial letters of those Hebrew words: *Torah, Nevi'im, Ketuvim. TNK.*
- *Torah:* The Five Books of Moses, Genesis to Deuteronomy.
- *Tzit-tzit (tsiytsith or tsee-tseeth):* Braided fringe of Numbers 15:38-40, put on the corners of one's garment.
- *YHVH:* The Name of the one true God is comprised of four Hebrew letters: *yod, hey, vav, hey:* יהוה. This Name is often translated as "God" or "Lord," but these are *titles* and not His Name. To indicate His Name, we use the four English letters that most closely resemble those Hebrew letters: YHVH.

BIBLIOGRAPHY

The following is a list of Abbreviations used for references purposes in this work.

BDB: *New Brown-Driver-Briggs-Gesenius Hebrew- Aramaic Lexicon*
NIV: *New International Version Study Bible*
Strong's: *Strong's Exhaustive Concordance*
S&BDB: *Strong's and Brown-Driver-Briggs together*
TWOT: *Theological Wordbook of the Old Testament*

The following is a listing of writings used in the making of this book.

Adler, Mortimer J. *Ten Philosophical Mistakes*. NY: Macmillian, 1997.
Aharoni, Yohanan; Michael Avi-Yonah. *The Macmillan Bible Atlas*. NY: Macmillan, 1977.
Bacchiocchi, Samuele. *From Sabbath To Sunday*. Maplewood NJ: Hammond, 1979, 2000.
Barna, George. *Revolution*. Tyndale House Publishers, Inc: Wheaton, IL, 2005.
Barraclough, Geoffrey. *Times Atlas of World History*. Pontifical Gregorian University Press: Rome, 1997.
Brown, Frances. *The New Brown-Driver-Briggs-Gesenius Hebrew- Aramaic Lexicon*. Peabody, MA: Hendrickson, 1998.
Carta's Historical Atlas of Israel. Jerusalem: Carta, 1983.
Cohen, A. Rev. Dr. *Ezekiel*. NY, London: Soncino, 1999.
Cohen, A. Rev. Dr. *Isaiah*. NY, London: Soncino, 1999.

Cohen, A. Rev. Dr. *The Twelve Prophets*. NY, London: Soncino, 1999.
DeHaan, M. R.. *The Chemistry of the Blood*. Grand Rapids: Zondervan, 1971, 1989.
Dowley, Tim. *The Kregal Pictorial Guide To The Bible*. Grand Rapids: Kregal Publications, 2000.
Eckstein, Yechiel, Rabbi. *What Christiand Should Know About Jews and Judaism*. Waco, TX: Word, 1984.
Edersheim, Alfred. *The Life and Times of Jesus the Messiah*. Grand Rapids: Eerdman's, 1979, 1997.
Edersheim, Alfred. *The Temple*. Grand Rapids: Kregal, 1997.
Edidin, Ben M. *Jewish Customs And Ceremonies*. NY: Hebrew Publishing, 1987.
Edidin, Ben M. *Encyclopaedia Judaica, 16 Vols*. Jerusalem: Keter, 1972.
Even-Shushan, Avraham. *New Concordance of the Tanach*. Jerusalem: Sivan, 1983, 1999.
Fay, Frededrick L. *A Map Book For Bible Students*. Old Tappan, NJ: Revell, 1966.
Fellner, Judith. *In the Jewish Tradition, A Year of Food and Festivities*. Middle Village, NY: Jonathan David Publishers. 1995.
Frank, Ephraim. *Return to the Land: An Ephraimite's Journey Home*. St. Cloud, FL: Key of David, 2004.
Frankel, Ellen, and Betsy Platkin Teutsch.*The Encyclopedia of Jewish Symbols*. Northvale, NJ: Jason Aronson Inc., 1992.
Gesenius' Hebrew-Chaldee Lexicon To The Old Testament. Grand Rapids. Baker, 1979, 2000.
Gilbert, Martin. *Atlas of Jewish History*. NY: William Morrow, 1993.
Gilbert, Martin. *Israel: A History*. NY: William Morrow, 1998.
Green, Jay P. *The Interlinear Bible*, Hebrew, Greek, English. Grand Rapids: Baker, 1979.
Gruber, Daniel. *Rabbi Akiba's Messiah*. Hanover, NH: Elijah Publishing House, 1999.
Harris, R. Laird, Gleason L. Archer Jr., and Bruce K. Waltke, eds. *Theological Wordbook of the Old Testament, 2 Vols*. Chicago: Moody, 1998.
Hatch, Edwin, and Henry A. Redpath. *Hatch and Redpath Concordance to the Septuagint, 2 Vols*. Grand Rapids: Baker, 1983.
Holladay, William L. Editor. *A Concise Hebrew and Aramaic Lexicon of The Old Testament*. Grand Rapids: Eerdman's, 1991.
House of David Herald. Lakewood, NY - White Stone, VA - Saint Cloud, FL: 1982-2000.
Interpreter's Dictionary of the Bible, 5 Vols. Nashville: Abingdon, 1983.
Jablonowski, Paul. *Sons to Glory*. www.sonstoglory.com: 2008.
Jahn, Herb. *The Aramic New Covenant*. Orange, CA: Exegeses, 1996.
Jenkins, Simon. *Bible Mapbook*. Herts, England: Lion, 1985.
Knapp, Christopher. *The Kings of Judah & Israel*. Neptune NJ: Loizeaux, 1983.
Kolatch, Alfred J. *The Jewish book of Why*. Middle Village NY: Jonathan David, 1981, 1995.

BIBLIOGRAPHY

Kolatch, Alfred J. *The Second Jewish Book of Why*. Middle Village NY: Jonathan David, 1996.

Isaacson, Ben, Dr. David Gross, ed. *Dictionary of the Jewish Religion* Englewood, NJ: Bantam, 1979.

Lamsa, George M. *The Holy Bible From Ancient Eastern Manuscripts*. Nashville: Holman, 1968, 1984.

Leil, C.F.; F. Delitzsch. *Commentary on the Old Testament In Ten Volumes*. Grand Rapids: Eerdman's, 1981.

Lisman, Lee. *What Kind of "Holiday Memories" Does God Have?*. P.O. Box 1501 Brush Prairie, WA 98606

Messianic Israel Herald. Saint Cloud, FL. 1999-2002.

Mordecai, Victor. *Is Fanatic Islam A Global Threat?* Jerusalem, 2002. Fifth Edition.

The New Encyclopaedia Britannica, 29 Vols. Chicago: Encyclopedia Britannica, 1985, 2003.

The New English Bible With the Apocrypha. Oxford, England: Oxford University Press, 1994.

New International Version Study Bible. Grand Rapids: Zondervan, 1985, 1995.

Newsome, James D. Jr., ed. *A Synoptic Harmony of Samuel, Kings and Chronicles*. Grand Rapids: Baker.

Norcross, Paul D. *Dining at the Master's Table*. 1997. Charlemont, MA. Kingdom Presence Publishing.

Pearl, Chaim, ed. *The Encyclopedia of Jewish Life and Thought*. Jerusalem: Carta, 1987.

Pfeiffer, Charles F., Howard F. Vos, John Rea, eds. *Wycliffe Bible Encyclopaedia*. Chicago: Moody, 1983.

Richards, Lawerence O. *Expository Dictionary of Bible Words*. Grand Rapids: Zondervan, 1985.

Scherman, Nosson, and Meir Zlotowitz, eds. *Genesis. ArtScroll Tanach Series*. Brooklyn: Mesorah, 1987.

Scherman, Nosson, and Meir Zlotowitz, Rabbis. *The Wisdom In The Hebrew Alphabet*. Brooklyn: Mesorah Publications, 1993.

Scherman, Nosson, and Meir Zlotowitz, Rabbis. *Stone Edition The Chumash*. Mesorah, 1993-2001.

Smith, Wallace E. *Are Christian Holidays... Holy Days?* Las Vegas: 2005.

Smith, Wallace E., and Wootten, Batya Ruth, *Israel— Empowered by the Spirit*. Saint Cloud, FL, Key of David Publishing: 2009.

Smith, Wallace E. *The Revelation of Yeshua, A First Century Look at a First Century Book*. Las Vegas: 2008

Smith, William, L.L.D. *Smith's Bible Dictionary*. Peabody, MA: Hendrickson, 1997.

Strong, James. *The New Strong's Exhaustive Concordance*. Nashville: Thomas Nelson, 1984, 2002.

Stern, David H. *Jewish New Testament Commentary*. Clarksville, MD: Jewish New Testament Pub. 1995.

TenBoom, Corrie, Sherrill, Elizabeth. *The Hiding Place*. Chosen Books, 1996.

Tenny, Merrill, ed. *Zondervan Pictorial Encyclopedia of the Bible*, 5 Vols. Grand Rapids: Zondervan, 1976.

Thayer, Joseph Henry. *Thayer's Greek-English Lexicon of the New Testament.* Grand Rapids: Baker, 1983.

Thomas, Winton, ed. *Documents from Old Testament Times.* New York: Harper & Row, 1961.

Turner, Nigel *Christian Words.* Nashville: Thomas Nelson, 1981.

Unger, Merrill F. *Unger's Bible Dictionary.* Chicago: Moody, 1974, 1996.

Vaughn, Curtis, ed. *26 Translations of the Holy Bible.* Atlanta: Mathis, 1985.

Vincent, Marvin R. *Vincent's Word Studies of the New Testament.* McLean, VA: MacDonald.

Vine, W.E. *Expanded Vine's Expository Dictionary of New Testament Words.* Minneapolis: Bethany, 1984.

Walton, John H. *Chronological Charts of the Old Testament.* Grand Rapids: Zondervan, 1978.

Webster's Third New International Dictionary, 3 Vols. Chicago: Encyclopedia Britannica, 1981.

Whiston, William, trs. *The Works of Flavius Josephus,* 4 Vols. Grand Rapids: Baker, 1974, 1992.

Wilson, William. *Wilson's Old Testament Word Studies, Unabridged Edition.* McLean, VA: MacDonald.

Wootten, Angus. *The Restoration of the Kingdom to Israel.* Saint Cloud, FL: Key of David, 2000.

Wootten, Angus. *Take Two Tablets.* Saint Cloud: Key of David, 2002.

Wootten, Batya Ruth. *Israel's Feasts and their Fullness: Expanded Edition.* Saint Cloud: Key of David, 2008.

Wootten, Batya Ruth. *Mama's Torah: The Role of Women.* Saint Cloud, FL: Key of David, 2004.

Wootten, Batya Ruth. *Redeemed Israel— Reunited and Restored* Saint Cloud: Key of David, 2006.

Wuest, Kenneth. *Weust's Word Studies From the Greek New Testament.* Grand Rapids: Eerdman's, 1981.

Yaniv, David. *Birth of the Messiah.* Lynnwood, WA: New West Press, Ltd. 1997.

Biography

Batya Wootten and her husband, Angus, were early pioneers in the Messianic movement. Decades ago they began publishing the first Messianic Materials Catalogue, created to serve a fledgling new interest in Israel and the Jewish people.

Batya read countless books about these subjects so she could write informed descriptions of them for the catalogue, and so discovered the great diversity of opinions about Israel's role in the world and about Israel's identity. Hungering to truly know the truth of the matter, she began to cry out in desperation to her Heavenly Father, asking Him to show her *His* truth. As promised, He answered: "Call to Me and I will answer you, and I will tell you great and mighty things, which you do not know" (Jer 33:3). The Holy One began to open up the Scriptures to her, and His answers led to the writing of many books about Israel and her full restoration.

Batya's challenging books represent decades of study, discussion, and prayer on the crucial issues of identifying Israel, celebrating her feasts, honoring Torah, and the role of women, and now— books about the role of the Holy Spirit, the Ruach haKodesh. Many readers have given testimony about having been transformed by her writings. Lives continue to be changed

The Voice... Hearing the Almighty

as they see the truth about Judah and Ephraim and their restoration. It is a truth that is helping to restore a brotherhood broken apart long ago. Her emphasis on the need to show mercy and grace to both houses is helping to heal the wounds that began when Israel was divided into two Kingdoms.

Her book, *Israel's Feasts and Their Fullness: Expanded Edition,* also represents many years of meticulous research, study, and prayerful writing. It is helping Believers to be liberated into glorious celebrations of the feasts. Several people have said of it, "This is the best book about the feasts that I have ever read." Her book, *Mama's Torah: The Role of Women,* has likewise received high acclaim from both men and women. She now offers the book you have in your hands, and a "companion" work: *Israel— Empowered by The Spirit,* by Wallace E. Smith and Batya Wootten.

And, there are more books yet to come.

Batya is married to her best friend, Col. Angus Wootten (Ret.), author of the visionary books, *Restoring Israel's Kingdom* and *Take Two Tablets Daily.* Together they have ten children who have blessed them with many beloved offspring.

Working as a team, Angus and Batya moved forward from the early days of the *House of David Catalogue* and began publishing a Newsletter, the *House of David Herald.* They also founded the informative Messianic Israel web site: *messianicisrael.com.* This led to the birth of the Messianic Israel Alliance— a rapidly growing and loosely affiliated Alliance of fellowships that agree with "The Hope of Messianic Israel," a broad statement of faith.

Together Angus and Batya publish books that serve the growing army of Believers who are discovering the truth about their Hebraic heritage. They work to help raise up new leaders and to draw out their giftings. For this assignment they have been uniquely prepared by the God of Abraham, Isaac, and Jacob. We know you will be blessed as you read their works.

Batya posts the following notice in all of her books:

> *The Word tells us to " let the one who is taught share all good things with him who teaches" (Gal 6:6). If through this book a good thing has been accomplished in your life, please write and share your good news with me.*
>
> *Batya Wootten, PO Box 700217, Saint Cloud, FL 34770*
> *e-mail: batya@mim.net*

KEY OF DAVID PUBLICATIONS

Redeemed Israel—Reunited and Restored by Batya Ruth Wootten Batya's inspiring books are causing a stir, even sparking a reformation. She clearly explains the truth about both houses of Israel (Isa 8:14), has helped many thousands to discover their Hebraic heritage, to understand Israel and the Church, and the Father's master plan for all Israel. She now encourages us to press on, to realize Torah's proper place in our lives, and to enter more fully into our latter-day call. This book offers an awesome overview of our full restoration. Includes maps, lists, charts, and helpful graphics. Paper, 256 pages. $14.95   ISBN 1-886987-17-3

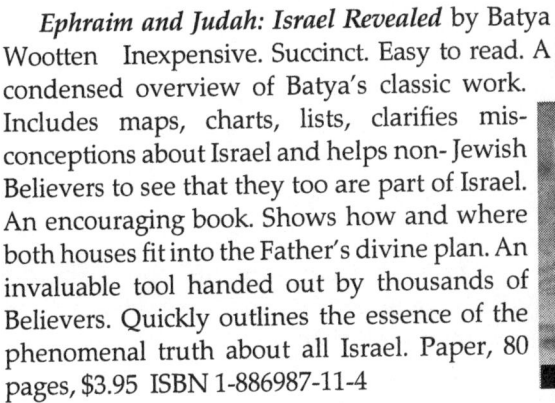

Ephraim and Judah: Israel Revealed by Batya Wootten Inexpensive. Succinct. Easy to read. A condensed overview of Batya's classic work. Includes maps, charts, lists, clarifies misconceptions about Israel and helps non-Jewish Believers to see that they too are part of Israel. An encouraging book. Shows how and where both houses fit into the Father's divine plan. An invaluable tool handed out by thousands of Believers. Quickly outlines the essence of the phenomenal truth about all Israel. Paper, 80 pages, $3.95 ISBN 1-886987-11-4

Spanish! Espanole: ¿Quién es Israel? The classic, *Who is Israel?* is available in Spanish. (Some maps and charts are in English only.) Offered at the special price of only $9.95   ISBN 1-886987-08-4

One Stick in His Hand Print by Crystal Lenhart Fine quality print, linen paper. Inspiring vivid sunset background in burgundy, red, blue, and purple tones. Size: 21x29" (3" white border, 15x23" image). Signed/numbered (1500 prints), $25.00. Not Signed, $15.00.

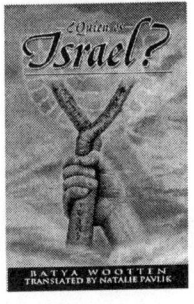

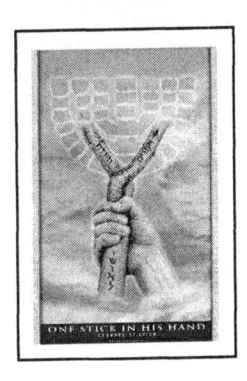

The Voice... Hearing the Almighty

Israel's Feasts and their Fullness: Expanded Edition by Batya Ruth Wootten This book is an informative, liberating classic. Written especially for those who understand about both houses of Israel, it is well researched, insightful, and highly enjoyable. Encourages freedom in Messiah, yet shows reverence for Scripture and due respect for Judaism's honorable traditions. Addresses Shabbat and the seven Feasts. Includes simple "Instruction Guides" for Sabbath, Havdalah, Passover, plus charts, tables, graphics. Batya's style has endeared her to many readers, and now she invites us to celebrate in the presence of the Almighty! Paper, 384 pages, $16.95   ISBN 1-886987-29-7

Passover in all its Fullness Includes Passover related chapters from the above book plus helpful Passover Guides. Explains the Four Passovers and the meaning of the Day of the Wave Sheaf. Makes an ideal gift at Passover celebrations. 96 pages, $4.95   ISBN 1-886987-15-7-3

Come! Let Us Rehearse the Four Passovers DVD! A dance filled two-hour drama narrated by Angus and Batya Wootten. Presents Passover based on Scripture. Depicts the four types of Passover (described in Batya's books): Family, Congregational, Personal, and Kingdom. Seeing Passover in dance and drama, while hearing related verses, is exciting, enlightening, encouraging. Watch this DVD and be inspired to celebrate Messiah's Passover like never before! DVD: $10.00

Package of Pamphlets— One Each: *Erev Shabbat, Havdalah, The Four Passovers, Messianic Jewish Passover,* and *Ten Days of Prayer* all by Batya Wootten. Each is printed on a folded 8 ½ x 11 size paper, and will fit nicely in your Bible. Five Pamphlets, $5.00.

Key of David Publications

The Voice... Hearing the Almighty by Batya Wootten Israel's Patriarchs all heard the voice of the Holy One and we should to. Man tends to fear hearing the Almighty and this book explains why. Yah said, *"In the latter days you will return to YHVH your God and listen to His voice"* (Deu 4:30). Difficult times are at our door, and we need to learn to hear His voice— now! Paper, 160 pages, $9.95 ISBN 1-886987-27-0

Israel— Empowered by The Spirit by Wallace E. Smith and Batya Ruth Wootten If you know about your Hebraic roots, yet long for a true move of the Holy Spirit, this book is for you! Finally, a book about the Ruach haKodesh for Messianics! It explains why we especially need the Holy Spirit, addresses counterfeit moves, prayer languages, prophecy, singing in the Spirit, words of wisdom and knowledge, gifts of healing, working of miracles, discerning of spirits, and deliverance. Offers a fascinating explanation of the Urim and Thummim of the High Priest and encourages us to release the Spirit within! An important handbook! Paper, 192 pages, $11.95   ISBN 1-886987-28-9

Mama's Torah: The Role of Women (NEW! Expanded Edition) by Batya Wootten This in-sightful book is getting rave reviews from men and women. Defines "helpmeet," delightfully depicts the roles of husband and wife, shows how women in Scripture were used, addresses difficult verses, unveils the call to women in this hour, especially in regard to the spirit of Torah. Paper, 160 pages, $9.95   ISBN 1-886987-20-3
Available on Audio CD!

Also Available in an Audio CD Set!
Redeemed Israel: Reunited and Restored!
Now you can *listen* to this anointed book!
Set of 6 CD's, $29.95

The Voice... Hearing the Almighty

Restoring the Kingdom to Israel by Angus Wootten This exciting new book replaces Angus' earlier work, *Restoring Israel's Kingdom*. Completely updated and greatly enlarged, it addresses Ezekiel's Temple and it asks, is Ezekiel's Temple destined to be built? Is there something in its description that we have missed? Does it have to do with Israel's final redemption? The chapters in this challenging book are titled: Keep Your Eye on the Goal. Defining the Kingdom Gospel. Ephraim's Punishment— and Full Restoration. The Way of the Gentiles. Gathering the Chosen Remnant. Ezekiel's Temple: It's Real Meaning. Lessons From History. The Messianic Vision. The Jubilee Generation. When Will Messiah Return? Preparing for The Final Battle. Paper, 256 pages, $14.95 ISBN 1-886987-26-2

Take Two Tablets Daily: The 10 Commandments and 613 Laws by Angus Wootten: The Laws of Moses were given to help Israel be strong, courageous, healthy, and blessed. This guide lists the 613 Laws of Jewish tradition as divided into Mandatory Commandments and Prohibitions, and lists the Scripture verse(s) from which each Law is derived. YHVH's Word is like medicinal ointment, and nothing is more symbolic of His Word than the two tablets on which He wrote His Covenant. Taken daily, these "Two Tablets" will give us life more abundantly. This reference book should be in every Believer's library. Paper, 96 pages, $4.95 ISBN 1-886987-06-8

New! A Door of Hope for the Last Days by Batya Ruth Wootten This book addresses the various "Rapture" theories and offers a unique perspective based on Scripture's "doors," on Messiah's comment about the "days of Noah," and on Israel's full restoration. Compelling and insightful, this work is causing many to rethink the end times. Paper, 160 pages, $9.95 ISBN 1-886987-32-7

KEY OF DAVID PUBLICATIONS

All Israel Dances Toward the Tabernacle by Chester Anderson and Tina Clemens Defines the dynamics of worship, answers dance-related questions: What is, and how did, dance originate? Does something special happen in the heavenlies when we dance? What attitude should have about it, and why? Why do I feel so drawn to Hebraic dance? Why is Davidic dance so popular? How does dance come into play in the restoration of both houses of Israel? This book will fill your heart with hope and it will set your feet a-dancin.' Paper, 192 pages, $12.95 ISBN 1-886987-09-2

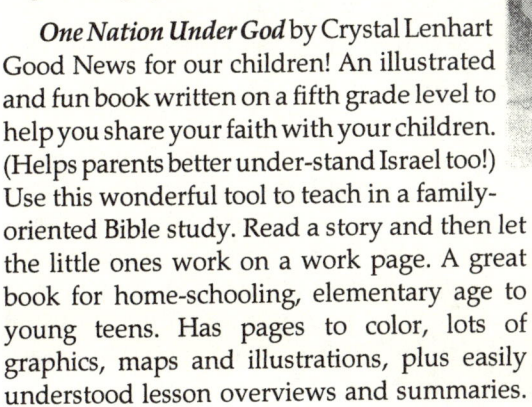

One Nation Under God by Crystal Lenhart Good News for our children! An illustrated and fun book written on a fifth grade level to help you share your faith with your children. (Helps parents better under-stand Israel too!) Use this wonderful tool to teach in a family-oriented Bible study. Read a story and then let the little ones work on a work page. A great book for home-schooling, elementary age to young teens. Has pages to color, lots of graphics, maps and illustrations, plus easily understood lesson overviews and summaries. Paper, Spiral Bound, 8x11, 76 pages, $12.00 ISBN 1-886987-16-5

My Beloved's Israel by Gloria Cavallaro
This personal journal that will help you: Deepen your relationship with your bridegroom, embark on an intimate journey into the heart of our Father, have a relationship with Him like David described, know intimacy with the bridegroom like that of the Song of Songs. Gloria chronicles her visions and dreams and interprets them in light of scriptural reflection. She concludes that Israel must be reunited if she is to be prepared for her latter-day challenges. Her exhortations help us prepare our hearts for the days ahead. Paper, 384 pages $16.95   ISBN 1-886987-05-X

The Voice... Hearing the Almighty

Return to the Land: An Ephraimite's Journey Home by Ephraim Frank As a new Believer, Ephraim could not explain what he felt burning in his soul. He only knew that he was being drawn, wooed by His God, and that he had gone on a tour that had forever changed his life... From the farm lands of America to the Holy Land of Israel, this compelling autobiography tells of a "stranger" who felt divinely drawn to both the Promised Land and the God of Abraham, Isaac, and Jacob. It tells of the birthing of a new and fresh move of the Holy One, gently reveals what the Father is doing in the Earth today, and tells of the blessed redemption of *all* Israel.

Paper, 240 pages, $12.95   ISBN 1-886987-18-1

Ruth and Esther: Shadows of our Future by Frank Morgan, M.D. The timeless love stories of Ruth and Esther speak of the elect. They tell of the divine destiny of Ephraim and Judah. In breath-taking fashion they reveal the redemption and restoration of all Israel. Morgan unveils the deep truths found in these stories of a widow and a maiden, both of whom were used mightily by God. Morgan gives us glimpses of the depth of Yah's great love for each of us, and provides insights into His latter-day plan for a redeemed Israel.
Paper, 144 pages, $9.95   ISBN 886987-19-X

Key of David books are distributed by:
Messianic Israel Marketplace
PO Box 3263, Lebanon, TN 37088
www.messianicisrael.com
1.800.829.8777

KEY OF DAVID
PUBLISHING
Unlocking *your* future...

Visit...
www.keyofdavidpublishing.com

Notes